Desserts
THE PERFECT
FINISH

Photography: Ashley Barber
Food Stylist: Voula Kyprianou

Published by Bay Books Pty Ltd
61-69 Anzac Parade
Kensington NSW 2033

Publisher: George Barber

National Library of Australia Card number and
ISBN 0 85835 967 7

BBC86

The publishers would like to thank the following companies for
their assistance during the photography of this book: The Bay Tree
Kitchen Shop, Breville, Bendigo Pottery, Ceramic Crafts (Argyle
Arts Centre), Crown Corningware, David Jones (Australia) Pty
Ltd, Hale Imports Pty Ltd, Kosta Boda, Mikasa Tableware, Peters
of Kensington, Pillvuyt, Saywell Imports, Slatecraft, Suomi and
Roden Products and Westinghouse (for microwave ovens).

Desserts
THE PERFECT
FINISH

Mary-Lou Arnold   Fiorella de Boos-Smith
Christine Heaslip   Douglas Marsland   Jan Wunderlich

Bay Books
Sydney & London

CONTENTS

Chocolate profiterole.

Feast your eyes and tempt your tastebuds with our exciting collection of desserts, ranging from the quickest fruit salad to crisp meringues, creamy mousses and fluffy souffles. A dessert, no matter how simple or spectacular, provides the finishing touch to any meal and is the one course that everyone eagerly awaits. With just a little planning and decoration, we show you how to make the dessert course the easiest and most spectacular part of the meal.

PLANNING AHEAD

When deciding which dessert to make for a lunch or dinner party take all factors into consideration. Firstly, how much time do you have? If you are busy with work or family, it is impractical to take on something too time consuming or ambitious, so decide on a dessert that is either quick to prepare or can be made in advance and kept in the fridge or freezer. Cook a tart beforehand and decorate it with fruit the day it is used, poach fruit in wine the night before and serve it cold or prepare a crumble which is ready to go straight into the oven when guests arrive.

What dishes will be served for the first two courses? Try to avoid using the same ingredients in more than one course, especially cream and eggs which tend to make a meal very rich. Think of a dessert which will balance and complement the entree and main course. If you serve a spicy main course consider a light, cooling dessert such as Banana Cream, or something fresh and tangy such as Pineapple Calypso (see recipes) which will offset the strong flavour of the spices. Follow a heavy meal like a stew with a refreshing sorbet or citrus souffle.

A freezer is an ideal companion for those who can prepare ahead. Make double batches of a dessert, such as sorbet or ice cream or prepare pie bases which can simply be defrosted as required. Fruit also freezes well and, if cooked into a sauce, is easy to store and takes up little space. Defrosted, it can be served over ice cream for a quick, fuss-free finish to a meal. There are many ways a freezer can be used to prepare ahead and this is covered in more detail on page 9.

If you have any last minute preparations, make sure that all your equipment is ready to use and all ingredients have been weighed out before guests arrive. Have the oven on at the correct temperature and arrange the shelves beforehand to avoid reshuffling them once they are hot and you are in a hurry.

Similarly, if you have any last minute decorating to do, prepare as much as possible before the dinner starts. Have any ingredients at room temperature and, if piping cream, whip it beforehand and keep it in the piping bag in the refrigerator so it's ready for immediate use.

Desserts are not just a dinner party occasion. More often than not, the family looks forward to a sweet treat to finish a meal. Family desserts are especially enjoyable because they include all the favourites such as Apple and Plum Crumble, Queen of Puddings and Rice Pudding (see recipes). Not only are they moreish but they provide the opportunity of using up excess fruit and ingredients which often leads to new dishes being created.

INSTANT DESSERTS

Sometimes the temptation for a dessert is a spur of the moment decision and with a few ingredients stocked away in the pantry you can create a number of delicious, interesting sweets. Try dried fruit soaked in sherry, or coconut cream melted into natural yoghurt as a quick sauce for fruit, or natural yoghurt pureed with dried apricots, spiced with cinnamon and topped with crushed pistachios.

THE PANTRY SHELF SHOPPING LIST

Nuts: Pistachio, walnuts, almonds, pecans, hazelnuts
Dried Fruit: Apricots, prunes, bananas, apples, sultanas, dates, coconut, prunes
Spices: Cinnamon, cloves, nutmeg, mixed spice
Assorted Ingredients: Dark chocolate, white chocolate, caster sugar, brown sugar, icing sugar, honey, natural yoghurt, ice cream, creamed coconut, canned fruit, marshmallows, rose water, frozen filo and puff pastry, golden syrup, treacle

PRODUCE

When buying fruit for a dessert, especially if it is to be served raw, buy only the best quality. Feel the fruit and select only firm, plump produce, avoiding any with bruised or discoloured skin. Avoid shrivelled produce or fruit that will be over-ripe by the time you want to serve it. Be adventurous: if a new fruit appears on the market, buy a small quantity of it and highlight it in a dish for the family, if it's a success then incorporate it into your repertoire for entertaining.

Take advantage of surplus fruit which is often available at low prices. Cook it in wine with spices such as cloves or cinnamon; poach it in a sugar syrup or puree it to make a fruit sauce. Any excess can be frozen and used later in a jelly, sorbet, ice cream or mousse.

DECORATIONS

A few simple decorations can turn a simple dessert into a spectacular course and, for the occasional mishap, hide a multitude of sins!

Feature one of the ingredients in the dessert as part of the decoration. With a citrus dessert for example, poach or caramelise some of the rind and sprinkle it over the finished dish. Cut fruit such as grapefruit, pineapple, orange or kiwi fruit so that the shell can be saved and used as a serving dish.

Jam glaze brushed over a fruit tart not only enhances the colour and gives it a shiny finish but also prevents the fruit from drying out. Alternatively, dip whole pieces of fruit, such as strawberries, mandarin segments or grapes first into a sugar syrup, dust with caster sugar for a frosted effect, then use them to decorate.

Chocolate is useful for decorating desserts as it is so easy to store and gives a number of different decorative finishes or coatings. For a quick garnish, shave chocolate off the block with a potato peeler or cut into long flakes to serve with ice cream. Paint melted chocolate onto leaves, then peel away the leaf leaving a perfect impression which can be used on gateaux, mousses or as a plate garnish. Coat cupcake moulds with chocolate, then peel away the casing and fill the cups with fresh fruit which has also been dipped in chocolate. This can either be served with coffee or topped with piped cream for a quick yet effective dessert.

The secret of successful desserts is to work with the ingredients you have or with produce in season, and adapt to fit the occasion. Anticipation is on your side, and family and friends will look forward to your experiments and discoveries with enthusiasm and delight.

Frosting grapes, this time dipping the fruit in whipped egg white before dusting with caster sugar

Painting melted chocolate onto ivy leaves

FREEZING HINTS

You can realise the full potential of your freezer by using it for storing desserts, puddings and cakes. Not only does it make sense to cook in bulk then stow, say, half a dozen of your favourite cheesecakes or apple pies, it also enables you to produce a mouth-watering but impressively complicated sweet at the drop of a hat.

If faced with the prospect of unexpected guests or in need of a dependable family favourite, it's then merely a matter of thawing one of your ready-made puds while your hands are free to prepare other courses.

Easiest options are, of course, those delicious home-made ice creams and meringues which require little or no thawing. They can be transformed into an exotic finale to any meal with the simple addition of fresh fruit, a little imaginative decoration or some piped cream.

Gelatine-based desserts: Souffles, chiffons and chilled cheesecakes need more cautious handling. A fairly high proportion of gelatine in the recipe means it's unlikely to freeze successfully, but you can gauge this with a little experimentation. Just save a slice of favourite cheesecake or souffle from one you're serving up and pop it in the freezer for a couple of weeks. If, after this time, it shrinks or takes on a leathery appearance you'll know it's not an exercise to repeat. Cooked cheesecakes, on the other hand, fare much better in the freezer. To preserve their appearance they can be frozen in their baking dish, but removed from this once solid and re-wrapped for longer-term storage. That frees your dish for repeated use.

Home-made pies and puddings: There's nothing like a home-made pie to make the mouth water, but every cook knows they're not turned out in a moment, so it makes sense to cook in bulk and keep a stock in the freezer. Pastry undoubtedly freezes better when uncooked and the pie should ideally be allowed an hour's thawing time. If you're in too much of a rush to thaw, remember to give your pie a few extra minutes in the oven — the timespan depends on its size.

Many of the traditional-style 'heavy' desserts like rice, sago and tapioca will freeze well, though they may thin down a little in the process. Steam puddings should be removed from the steamer as soon as they're cooked, then chilled rapidly, wrapped and frozen, while accompanying sauces should be thickened **after** thawing.

Peeling away the leaf for a perfect impression

Stacking crepes before sealing in bags and freezing

Pancakes: Pancakes are extremely versatile, for both sweet and savoury recipes, but it's important to recognise which types will freeze most effectively. Thin French-style crepes made with eggs will keep very well at icy temperatures, but thick pancakes and those containing little or no egg lose pliability, become tough and will crack. For best results you should place freezer sheeting between each crepe and pack a stack of them in well-sealed freezing bags, having removed as much air as possible from the container. Thaw the crepes at room temperature before filling them.

Cakes: Few people have time these days for the weekly cake-baking session undertaken by our mothers and grandmothers, but with the traditional Victoria sponge still a firm family favourite, the answer's simple — keep a frozen cake store.

An unfilled sponge cake will keep successfully for up to four months in a sealed freezer bag with as much air as possible removed beforehand.

The trick in freezing all cakes is to chill them **unwrapped** until firm, then put them in airtight containers. Filled sponges will keep up to a month in a lidded container and may be sliced into servings before freezing to speed up the thawing process and save you having to defrost an entire cake when just a couple of slices are needed.

Freezer storage space is often at a premium so a handy tip to remember is to save decoration of cakes and desserts until they're thawed. If you don't, you'll find that valuable space is taken up by bulky containers protecting your handiwork, or alternatively you'll be unable to stack other dishes on top of frail confections.

Fruitful freezing: With so many delicious fruits enjoying a very short season, it makes sound economic sense to buy them when they're available at low cost and store them in the freezer. However, use the wrong chilling technique and all your cost cutting methods could go to waste. There are three foolproof methods of storing fruit. Firstly, you can preserve fruits in a syrup pack, with one of three strengths. For a thin syrup, use one cup of sugar to three cups of water; for a medium syrup add one cup of sugar to two cups of water and a thick syrup is made from equal proportions of sugar and water. Then it's simply a matter of boiling the water until the sugar is completely dissolved into it, and allowing the solution to cool. It should then be gently poured over fruit, packed into a rigid container, just 2 cm short of the top. The syrup should cover the fruit completely, but not entirely fill the container, as liquid expands when frozen.

The second method of storage is dry sugar packing, which involves dipping the fruit into a protective mixture made of the juice of one lemon and two cups of water. Fruit should be drained, dipped once, then sprinkled with sugar and placed in a sealed, airtight freezer bag. This method is, however, only suitable for fruits that will not discolour.

As many of us prefer to keep our fruit sugar-free for diet or health reasons, the third method of storage — using an unsugared or artificially sweetened solution — is a good alternative.

You simply place a freezer bag in a rigid container, then half-fill it with fruit which has been dipped in the protective solution (made from the juice of one lemon to two cups of water). The fruit should then be covered with an unsugared pack solution (one tablespoon of ascorbic acid per 5 cups of water) which may be artificially sweetened if you prefer. Squeeze as much air as possible from the bag, then seal it, and put a lid on the container.

As a rule of thumb, remember that any fruits you find in cans can generally be frozen successfully. However, don't overstretch yourself when embarking on a fruit-freezing operation — prepare too many fruits like peaches, nectarines and pears at one go and you'll find they discolour before you can complete the job. Also, many fruits do not need extensive preparation before freezing — all berry fruits, cherries and rhubarb, for instance, can be free frozen until solid then vacuum packed for longer term and space-saving storage.

Just one final word — before putting any of your frozen fruit packs into the freezer, do take the trouble to label them with the date and details of the contents — it will save much confusion when the time comes to thaw and use them!

A NOTE TO MICROWAVE USERS

Those cooks who use a microwave oven will be pleased to note that a selection of microwave desserts has been included at the end of each chapter with illustrations to show special techniques.

Please read the notes on Wattage and Standing Time carefully to ensure that you have successful results each time.

A range of special microwave equipment including decorative moulds and pie dishes is available from most department stores and we have listed the basic items required for cooking desserts below. If you do not wish to buy extra equipment try experimenting with the containers you have to achieve different shapes and effects. However, be careful not to use any metal dishes or dishes with any type of metallic decoration.

BASIC EQUIPMENT FOR SUCCESSFUL MICROWAVE DESSERTS

Item	Use
20 x 20 cm square dish	Cakes, slices, confectionery.
Browning casserole dish	Baking scones.
Casserole lid	Pavlovas, pies, quiches, cheese cakes and for cooking small quantities of food.
Ring dish	Baked custards, breads, scone rings, cakes.
Flan ring	Cheese cakes, fruit flans, quiches.

STANDING TIME

Standing time allows heat concentrated at the outer edge of the food to be conducted to the centre and for the cooking process to be completed. Food can remain covered and standing time can be allowed in the microwave (on a warm setting only) or dishes can be removed from the microwave. Standing time is usually one-third to one-half of the cooking time.

CLEANING

Always clean the oven with detergent and warm water after use. Remove all food splatters from the door and oven cavity and dry thoroughly with a clean dry cloth. Strong odours can be removed by placing a sprig of rosemary into the oven and microwaving on high for 2–3 minutes.

WATTAGE

Recipes included in this book can be cooked in 600 and 650 watt ovens. If you are using a 500 watt oven add a few minutes to the suggested cooking times.

TESTING FOR DONENESS

☐ Cakes leave the sides of the dish when cooked and any moist spots on the surface will dry during standing time.

☐ Test baked custard by inserting a knife into the custard ⅓ in from the edge. The knife, when withdrawn, should be clean. When cooking is complete stand cooked custard in cold water to cool and to halt the cooking process.

A range of microwave-safe cookware from Crown Corning

FRUITY DESSERTS

The simplicity and natural beauty of fruit makes it one of nature's most enjoyable ingredients to work with. Try your hand at the tempting collection of desserts in this chapter, adapting the recipes to suit the fruit in season and adding your own ideas to create more new and exciting desserts.

Fruit Salad in Cointreau

Mango Brown Betty

60 g butter
1 cup grated fresh coconut
2 cups half-ripe, sliced
    mango
¾ cup brown sugar
1 teaspoon cinnamon
3 tablespoons liquid from
    coconut

Melt butter and mix with coconut. Place a layer of coconut in greased ovenproof dish then add a layer of mangoes. Mix sugar and cinnamon together and sprinkle over mangoes. Repeat layers ending with coconut. Spoon over coconut liquid. Bake at 180°C (350°F) for 1 hour until mangoes are soft. Serve with lime sauce.

Serves 6

Note: To prepare a fresh coconut, puncture the three eyes with a screwdriver. Drain out the liquid (this is not the milk), then crack the shell with a rolling pin. Using a small, sharp knife, prise the flesh away from the skin, then peel off the tough brown covering with a potato peeler. Shred the white flesh or grind it in a blender.

Lime Sauce

1 tablespoon cornflour
½ cup sugar
¼ cup cold water
¾ cup boiling water
40 g butter
2½ tablespoons lime juice

Combine cornflour and sugar and mix to a paste with cold water. Gradually stir mixture into boiling water, stirring continuously until thickened. Add butter and lime juice and mix well.

Makes 1½ cups

Spiced Rhubarb

500 g rhubarb, sliced
⅓ cup sultanas
⅓ cup raisins
⅓ cup currants
1 teaspoon mixed spices
1 teaspoon cinnamon
¼ cup brown sugar
½ cup apricot juice
1 cup sweet white wine

Mix rhubarb, dried fruits and spices and place in greased shallow ovenproof dish. Heat sugar in apricot juice until dissolved. Add wine and pour over fruit. Cover and bake at 135°C (270°F) for 30–35 minutes.

Serves 4

Cherry Soup

This soup can also be served as an unusual finale at a dinner party. If cherries are not in season, use blueberries or raspberries instead.

500 g black ripe cherries,
    stoned
3 cups water
½ cup sugar
⅓ cup lemon juice
fresh mint for garnish
1 × 200 mg carton natural
    yoghurt (optional)

Bring cherries, water, sugar and lemon juice to the boil. Simmer gently for 10 minutes. Allow to cool. Puree in blender or food processor.
   Chill thoroughly. Serve garnished with mint and, if liked, a teaspoon of yoghurt in each bowl.

Serves 6

Note: This recipe may also be served over crushed ice.

Mango Brown Betty

1. *Place a layer of melted butter and coconut in a greased ovenproof dish*

2. *Top the butter and coconut with a layer of mangoes*

3. *Combine sugar and cinnamon and sprinkle over mangoes*

Melon and Berry Ambrosia

1 rock melon
1 honeydew melon
2 tablespoons honey
250 g black or green grapes
2 1/3 cups white wine
1 tablespoon rose water

Cut a slice from the top of each melon and remove the seeds. With a melon baller, scoop out the flesh and reserve in a bowl. Wash the grapes, remove any stems and add to the melon balls.

Mix the wine, honey and rose water together and pour it over the fruit. Leave to marinate in the fridge for several hours or overnight. Spoon into individual serving dishes and leave at room temperature for an hour before serving.

Serves 12

Note: If wished, the melons can be hollowed out and used as serving containers. Cut the edges into a scalloped border, place on a serving tray and surround with fresh flowers such as frangipani or hibiscus.

Fruit in Vermouth

1/2 cup sweet vermouth
1/4 cup sugar
1/4 teaspoon cinnamon
1 pineapple, cored and sliced
3 oranges, segmented
250 g green grapes, halved
   and seeded

Combine vermouth, sugar and cinnamon. Chill in refrigerator about 1 hour.

Place fruit in serving bowl and strain liquid over fruit. Chill at least 1 hour in refrigerator.

Serves 6–8

Serving Suggestion: This dessert can also be served with a non-alcoholic dressing such as: orange juice and cloves, sparkling apple juice instead of the vermouth or with a sugar syrup flavoured with rose water.

Caramelised Oranges

1/4 cup sugar
40 g butter
4 large oranges (navels)
4 tablespoons slivered
   almonds, toasted

Dissolve sugar over low heat, stirring constantly, and simmer until syrup is a golden colour. Remove from heat; add butter and stir until smooth. Peel the oranges, removing all pith and white membrane. Slice thinly and arrange on a serving dish in overlapping layers. Pour the sauce over them and sprinkle with almonds. Serve with whipped cream, if wished.

Serves 4

Berry Ambrosia

Chinese Pears

4 ripe pears
1 cinnamon stick
4 cloves
3 tablespoons chopped
  walnuts
3 tablespoons chopped dates
2 tablespoons honey
2 teaspoons ground ginger
slivered almonds

Peel pears, cut in half lengthwise and remove core. Place in baking dish, cut side up, with cinnamon and cloves. Combine walnuts, dates, honey and ginger to make a paste, fill pear cavities. Place pears in baking dish with a little water, cover with foil and bake at 180°C (350°F) until pears are tender. Serve sprinkled with toasted slivered almonds.

Makes 8 serves

Feijoa Compote

Raspberry Marlow

1½ cups raspberries
125 g marshmallows
⅓ cup fresh dates, thinly
  sliced
1 cup cream, whipped

Crush raspberries thoroughly. Heat with marshmallows over hot water until marshmallows melt. Add dates and refrigerate until cold. Fold in whipped cream and leave in freezer until frozen.

Serves 6

Feijoa Compote

¼ cup sugar
¾ cup water
¼ cup red wine
6 feijoas, peeled and halved
  lengthways
1 tablespoon cornflour
1 tablespoon water

Dissolve sugar in water and wine over low heat. Add feijoas and simmer for a few minutes until cooked but not mushy. Lift feijoas out and arrange in serving dish. Mix cornflour and water to a smooth paste and stir into syrup. Bring to boil and cook, stirring, until thickened. Spoon over fruit.

Serves 4

Apricot Sauce

1 cup dried apricots
1 cup water
2 tablespoons sugar
1 tablespoon lemon juice
¼ teaspoon cinnamon or
  nutmeg to taste

Soak apricots in just enough water to cover for 30 minutes. Drain and simmer 30 minutes in 1 cup water combined with lemon juice, sugar and cinnamon. Puree, reheat and serve with puddings such as Spotted Dick.

Makes about 1 cup

1. Dissolve sugar in water and wine over low heat

2. Add feijoas and simmer until cooked

3. Mix cornflour and water to a smooth paste and stir into syrup

16

Grape Custard

Once you have perfected the art of making a good custard, which is based generally on eggs and milk, you can flavour it and use it in countless ways with fruit, pastries, cakes and trifles, chilling it in the refrigerator and serving it as a refreshing finish to a good meal. This unusual custard is made with sweet white wine and garnished with frosted grapes.

2 cups sweet white wine
grated rind 1 lemon
6 egg yolks
1/4 cup caster sugar
2½ tablespoons cornflour
2 tablespoons water
4 egg whites
pinch salt
juice 1 lemon
225 g white muscat grapes
225 g black grapes
3 tablespoons brandy

Garnish

2 egg whites
3 tablespoons caster sugar

Boil the white wine and lemon rind for 2 minutes. Blend the egg yolks with half of the sugar. Mix in the cornflour and water. Gradually stir in the hot wine, then pour back into the saucepan and bring to the boil, stirring until thick. Remove from the heat.

Whisk the egg whites and salt until they form stiff peaks. Add the rest of the sugar and beat until thick. Fold into the warm custard with the lemon juice.

Reserve 18 white and black grapes for decoration. Halve and deseed the remaining grapes. Macerate them in the brandy.

Beat the egg whites for the garnish and dip the rims of 6 tall glasses into the mixture. Then dip into the sugar. Dip the grapes into the beaten egg whites and sugar, and chill.

Divide the grapes between the glasses. Top up with the custard mixture and chill for at least 2 hours. Decorate with the grapes.

Serves 6

Figs in Ouzo

500 g figs
1/4 cup Ouzo
cream, for serving

Remove stalks from figs and halve, but do not peel. Arrange in dish and pour over Ouzo. Chill thoroughly and serve with cream.

Serves 4

Grape Custard

Fruit Salad Kebabs

1 red-skinned apple, cubed
250 g fresh pineapple
   wedges
1 can mandarin segments,
   drained
250 g assorted melon balls or
   cubes
1 firm banana, sliced in 2 cm
   pieces
8 strawberries

Glaze

1 tablespoon cornflour or
   arrowroot
1/8 teaspoon cinnamon
1/4 cup strained lemon juice
1/4 cup strained orange juice
3 tablespoons honey　　　　　　　　　　　TIME: 6 MINUTES

Combine glaze ingredients in bowl. Place in oven and cook on
HIGH 2–3 minutes or until thick, stirring twice. One teaspoon
freshly chopped mint may be added.

Select a range of seasonal and canned fruits to make a colourful kebab.

Thread fruit on wooden sticks and brush with glaze. Arrange
in shallow dish. Heat on HIGH 2–3 minutes or until hot. Serve.

Serves 6–8

Baked Fruit with Orange Cream

3/4 cup cream
6 tablespoons sour cream
1 tablespoon icing sugar,
   sifted
grated rind 1 orange
3 teaspoons cinnamon
4 tablespoons brown sugar
juice 1 orange
juice 1 lemon
8 peaches, peeled, halved
   and stoned
8 plums, halved and stoned
8 apricots, halved and stoned

2 pears, peeled, cored and
   quartered
4 bananas, peeled and cut in
   large slices
3 tablespoons brandy

To make orange cream, whip cream and fold in sour cream,
icing sugar, orange rind and 1 teaspoon cinnamon. Cover and
chill.

Stir brown sugar into orange and lemon juice and remaining
cinnamon. Add all fruit and toss in sugar mixture until coated,
using hands. Refrigerate for 1 hour.

Drain fruit and arrange on 8 long skewers.

Place a large sheet of foil in baking dish. Lay kebabs in single
layer on foil then fold ends over to make a sealed parcel. Bake
at 190°C (375°F) for 20–25 minutes.

Arrange kebabs on serving dish. Heat brandy, ignite and
pour over fruit while still flaming. Serve with orange cream.

Serves 8

Fruit Salad Kebabs

Fresh Fruit Salad

2 oranges
2 mandarins
2 apples, peeled and diced
1 cup fresh strawberries
3 ripe pears
225 g grapes
3 bananas

Sugar Syrup

⅓ cup sugar
1 strip lemon rind, or piece
   of vanilla pod
5 tablespoons water
2–3 tablespoons liqueur such
   as kirsch, or maraschino
   (optional)

First prepare sugar syrup: dissolve sugar slowly in the water, add lemon rind or vanilla pod, and boil for 1 minute. Tip into a bowl and leave to cool.

Cut peel, pith and first skin from oranges with a sharp serrated-edged knife to expose flesh; then remove segments by cutting between each membrane. Peel and slice mandarins. Dice apples. Prepare strawberries. Peel and quarter pears, remove core, cut each quarter into two.

Pip grapes by hooking out pips with eye of a trussing needle or knife tip. Only white grapes should be peeled, not black ones. If skin is difficult to remove from white grapes, dip them into boiling water for 1 minute. Peel bananas and cut in thick, slanting slices.

Mix fruit and moisten with sugar syrup, add liqueur and turn fruit over carefully. Set a plate on top to keep fruit covered by the syrup. Chill before serving. Serve with whipped cream and almond tuile biscuit.

Serves 6–8

Bananas Caribbean

6 bananas
¼ cup brown sugar
½ cup orange juice
grated rind 1 orange
¼ teaspoon cinnamon
¼ teaspoon nutmeg
½ cup sherry
30 g butter
4 tablespoons rum

Peel bananas and arrange in flat, greased baking dish. Combine brown sugar, orange juice and rind, cinnamon, nutmeg and sherry in saucepan. Heat to dissolve sugar then spoon over bananas. Dot with butter. Bake at 180°C (350°F) for 10–15 minutes until tender. Just before serving, heat rum, set alight and pour over bananas.

Serves 6

Fruit Salad in Cointreau

1 mango, peeled and
   chopped
¼–½ cup Cointreau
6 red plums, stoned and
   chopped
6 strawberries, quartered
3 apricots, stoned and
   chopped
pulp 3 passionfruit
1 lime, peeled and chopped
1 banana, peeled and sliced
1 kiwifruit, peeled and sliced
1 apple, cored and diced
1 rock melon, seeded and
   scooped out with melon
   baller
1 guava, chopped

Marinate mango in small bowl with Cointreau for several hours. Puree in blender or food processor. Prepare remaining fruit, and combine with puree. Chill thoroughly.

Serves 6

Serving Suggestion: If wished, this recipe could be served in grapefruit or orange shells and the fruit included in the salad.

Banana Fritters

1 cup flour
pinch salt
1 egg, beaten
1 small can evaporated milk
4 bananas
1 cup cooking oil
½ cup caster sugar

Sift flour and salt into a bowl. Make a well in the centre of the flour, and into this pour the beaten egg. Blend the egg with the flour a little at a time by stirring in gradually increasing circles from the centre. As mixture thickens, add milk gradually, while continuing to stir, to form a smooth batter.

Allow to stand for 30 minutes.

Split bananas in half lengthwise.

Heat oil in frying pan over moderate heat.

Dip bananas in the batter and deep fry until golden brown. Remove, drain well, and roll in caster sugar. Serve with cream.

Serves 4

Candied Chestnuts

This is the Japanese version of marrons glaces. Cooking time is short, but the total preparation can take much longer. The addition of a little mirin (a sweet cooking sake) or sherry makes an interesting variation.

*500 g raw chestnuts, shelled
    and peeled*

Syrup

*1¼ cups sugar
2 cups water
2–3 dried gardenia pods or 1
    drop yellow food
    colouring*

Cut the base of each peeled chestnut off and trim body into an attractive shape. Soak chestnuts in cold water for at least 30 minutes to remove bitterness.

Make the syrup by combining the sugar and water and bringing slowly to the boil over a medium heat. Boil until the syrup is reduced by about 10 per cent. Cool.

Drop the raw chestnuts into water with the cracked gardenia pods or yellow food colouring and bring to the boil over a high heat. Reduce to a gentle simmer and cook for a further 20 minutes or until tender. Cool nuts under cold running water and drain. Discard pod.

Return chestnuts to a pan and pour over the syrup. Cover and simmer gently for 1 hour. Allow to cool overnight. Serve at room temperature. Serve 2–3 each on individual serving plates accompanied by fresh fruit.

Serves 8

Candied Chestnuts

Orange Ice

2 cups orange juice
½ cup lemon juice
1½ cups sugar
3 cups water
1 tablespoon orange-blossom
   water

Combine orange and lemon juices. Place sugar and water in a saucepan, bring to boil, simmer for 5 minutes and cool.

Stir in fruit juices, and orange-blossom water. Pour into refrigerator trays, cover with foil and freeze. As ice freezes a little, beat lightly with a fork to reduce crystal size. Repeat at 30 minute intervals. Transfer from freezer to refrigerator 20 minutes before serving.

Note: May be served in scooped-out orange shells or in glasses or shallow bowls. Garnish it with shredded lemon or orange peel, or both, or with thin slices of orange or melon.

Serves 4

Fruit with Strawberry Cream Dressing

This delicate, shell pink dressing is quick to make and can be served with any fruit in season. It is an ideal dessert to serve after a heavy meal or to finish a light luncheon.

1 tablespoon honey
2 cups natural yoghurt
nutmeg to taste
½ cup crushed strawberries
selection of seasonal fruit
   such as: lychees, apricots,
   plums, peaches, figs,
   dates, melon balls,
   mandarin segments,
   coconut squares

Mix together the honey and yoghurt, then season to taste with freshly grated nutmeg. Fold in the crushed strawberries and chill until required. Arrange the fruit on a serving platter with the dressing in the centre.

Serves 4–6

Note: Try different variations to the dressing, add crushed walnuts or pistachios, stir in desiccated coconut or even fold in a little melted creamed coconut.

Orange Ice

Fresh Fruit with Lemon Yoghurt Dressing

A tangy oil free dressing which is delicious served with fresh fruit. The fruit used in this recipe is merely a suggestion — it can be varied with whatever fruit is in season. This dessert is particularly good served with a spicy curry or sate, following chicken or quiche at lunch or simply served with champagne for a special brunch.

cup natural yoghurt	1 pawpaw
finely grated rind and juice	200 g green grapes
½ lemon	1 punnet strawberries
2 tablespoons freshly	½ rock melon
chopped mint	½ honeydew melon
2 tablespoons honey	

Mix the yoghurt, lemon rind and juice, mint and honey together in a bowl. Cover and leave in the fridge overnight. Cut the pawpaw into wedges. Wash and prepare the grapes and strawberries and, using a melon baller, scoop out the melon into balls.

Stand the dressing at room temperature to remove the chill. Arrange the fruit on the pawpaw slices, spoon the dressing over and serve.

Serves 4–6

Praline Powder

A crunchy garnish for all sweet mousses or ice cream.

½ cup caster sugar
½ cup roughly chopped
   blanched almonds

Melt sugar slowly in small saucepan. Do not stir. Roughly chop almonds in processor and add to sugar. Cook until golden, then stir with metal spoon until a good nut brown. Pour immediately on to well oiled baking tray. When cold, break up and place in processor with double blade and grind to a powder. Store in airtight jar and use as required.

Fresh Fruit with Lemon Yoghurt Dressing

1. *Stir boiled milk into eggs*

2. *Add vanilla and gelatine and stir until dissolved*

3. *Cook guavas in lemon juice and sugar until just tender*

Guava Mousse

1 tablespoon gelatine
2 tablespoons warm water
4 eggs
½ cup sugar
1 cup milk
1 teaspoon vanilla essence
500 g guavas, peeled and
   sliced

juice 1 lemon
1 tablespoon sugar
150 mL cream, whipped
1 guava and 1 kiwifruit,
   sliced for garnish

Dissolve gelatine in water. Beat eggs with sugar until light and fluffy. Boil milk and stir into eggs. Cook mixture over low heat until it coats the back of a wooden spoon. Add vanilla and gelatine and stir to dissolve. Leave in refrigerator until mixture thickens slightly.

Cook guavas in lemon juice and 1 tablespoon sugar until just tender. Cool slightly and puree in blender or food processor. Strain and discard seeds.

Fold cream into custard mixture with guavas. Taste and add more sugar if necessary. Pour into greased mould, cover and refrigerate for 6 hours until set. To serve, unmould onto serving platter and garnish with sliced guava and kiwifruit slices.

Serves 4

Chocolate-Avocado Swirl

1 large avocado
1 teaspoon vanilla essence
2 teaspoons honey
1 cup whipped cream
40 g dark chocolate, melted
30 g dark chocolate curls

Mash avocado with vanilla and honey. Fold through whipped cream. Slowly pour cooled, melted chocolate into avocado cream. Stir in slightly so as to give a streaky look. Spoon into tall parfait glasses and garnish with curls.

Serves 2

Note: To accentuate the chocolate swirl, use a piping bag with a very fine attachment and make a spiral design on the inside of the glass. Allow to set and gently spoon in avocado mixture.

Apricot Mousse

500 g ripe apricots
juice ½ lemon
3 tablespoons icing sugar
2 teaspoons gelatine
½ cup cream
toasted slivered almonds

Plunge apricots into boiling water and leave 1 minute. Drain, cover with cold water to cool. Peel. Cut apricots in half and remove stones. Puree apricots with lemon juice and sugar in a blender or sieve.

Place gelatine in ¼ cup cold water and stand over bowl of hot water until dissolved. Stir into apricot puree. Beat cream until stiff, fold into apricot mixture. Spoon into individual serving dishes and refrigerate until set. Serve garnished with toasted almond slivers.

Serves 4–6

Note: Canned apricots may be used if well drained.

Frozen Fruit Mousse

Any fruit in season can be used such as mangoes, peaches, pears or apricots. Liqueur can be added if desired.

2 cups prepared fruit
4 egg yolks
1½ cups sugar
1–2 cups whipped cream

Puree fruit. Whip sugar and egg yolks together over bain-marie until thick. Add to pulp in food processor and blend. Add whipped cream and blend in short bursts on PULSE for 2–3 seconds. Freeze in trays for 1–1½ hours.

Serves 4

Guava Mousse

French Avocado Gateau

A choux pastry served in a spectacular symphony of greens.

2 cups water
6 tablespoons butter
2 tablespoons raw sugar
2 cups flour
8 eggs

Filling

2 small bunches green
  grapes, seedless
2 cups stiffly whipped cream
3 avocados, beaten with 4
  tablespoons honey until
  smooth and creamy

Chop butter into small pieces and melt it with the water and sugar. Bring to the boil and remove from heat. Add flour all at once and stir vigorously.

Return to heat and cook further over moderate heat until pastry forms a ball.

Remove from heat and stir in eggs, one at a time, beating well.

Grease and flour 3 × 20 cm round pie dishes. Divide mixture equally between the dishes and spread evenly over, leaving about 2 cm between edge of pie dish and pastry. Bake at 180°C (350°F) for 20 minutes. Turn oven off and leave in further 5 minutes. Remove from oven and cool.

Mix avocado and honey with whipped cream until blended. Pull grapes from stems and wash well.

To serve, spread each choux ring with avocado cream and decorate with grapes. Put the layers of choux pastry onto each other to form a gateau. Pipe a little avocado cream around the edge of the top ring. Cut into cake wedges.

Serves 8

Avocado Yoghurt Dessert Loaf

Weight-conscious people will love this healthful, yoghurt-based, ice cream loaf.

400 g low-fat natural
  yoghurt
2 tablespoons honey
1 large avocado
½ teaspoon vanilla essence
2 teaspoons grated orange
  rind
1 egg white

Mash avocado with a little of the yoghurt or blend until smooth. Combine the remaining yoghurt, honey, vanilla essence and orange rind with the avocado and mix well.

Pour into loaf tray and freeze for about 1 hour, or until mixture is beginning to set. Beat ice cream to mix in the ice crystals. Beat egg white until stiff and fold gently into ice cream. Return to freezer after smoothing ice cream evenly on top. Freeze until set.

Serves 4

Baked Honey Pears

4 firm pears
4 tablespoons chopped dates
2 tablespoons chopped
    walnuts   Combine
3 tablespoons honey
¼ teaspoon cinnamon   TIME: 8 MINUTES

Peel pears. Cut off caps 2.5 cm from top. Core each pear without cutting right through. Remove seeds. Fill centres with date mixture, replace caps. Arrange in a circle on a glass plate and cook on HIGH 6–8 minutes.

Pears can be served whole: remove cap and top with whipped cream, or cut in half, served with a rosette of whipped cream.

Serves 4

Note: If pears are not in season, experiment with other fruit such as peaches, apricot or apple.

Peaches Flambe

30 g butter
1 × 425 g can drained peach
    halves
2 tablespoons Grand Marnier
1½ tablespoons sugar
3 extra tablespoons Grand
    Marnier for flaming   TIME: 5½ MINUTES

Heat butter in glass serving dish for 1–2 minutes. Add peach halves and Grand Marnier. Sprinkle with sugar and cook 3 minutes on HIGH. Heat extra Grand Marnier in glass jug for 25 seconds, flame and pour over peaches. Serve with vanilla ice cream.

Serves 4

Strawberry Cream

2 punnets ripe red
    strawberries
4 eggs, separated
1 tablespoon gelatine
8 tablespoons sugar
1 × 30 mL carton cream,
    whipped   TIME: 7 MINUTES

Wash and hull strawberries. Puree 1½ punnets. Blend puree, egg yolks, gelatine and sugar. Place in a bowl and cook on DEFROST 7 minutes until gelatine dissolves, stirring constantly.

Chill until slightly set. Beat cream to form stiff peaks. Fold into strawberry puree and beaten egg whites. Pour into individual glass sweet dishes to set. Decorate with whipped cream and remaining strawberries.

Serves 6–8

Pears with Chocolate Sauce

6 firm pears
1 tablespoon lemon juice,
    strained
¼ cup sugar
2 tablespoons dry sherry
2 tablespoons Grand Marnier
180 g cooking chocolate
    pieces
40 g butter   TIME: 14 MINUTES

Peel pears, leaving stems intact. Remove core from the base by cutting a circle with paring knife. Brush with lemon juice to prevent discolouring.

In a 1 litre casserole combine sugar, sherry and Grand Marnier. Place pears on sides with the thicker ends towards the outside. Add remaining lemon juice and cover. Cook on HIGH for 6 minutes. Turn pears over and baste. Cover and cook a further 6 minutes or until tender. Remove pears. Reserve poaching liquid.

Measure ½ cup poaching liquid and return to casserole. Add cooking chocolate pieces and cook on HIGH 2 minutes. Add butter and whisk till smooth.

Fill each pear with custard sauce. Place upright on serving dish. Pour remaining custard around pears and spoon chocolate sauce over top.

Serves 6

Seasonal Fruit Selection

½ cup frozen berries
¼ cup shredded coconut
2 tablespoons finely chopped
    pecans
1 × 300 mL carton sour
    cream
2 tablespoons fresh cream or
    milk
assorted fresh fruit wedges
almond macaroons
pink and white marshmallow
    halves
lemon juice, strained   TIME: 4 MINUTES

Place frozen berries into bowl. Cook on HIGH 4 minutes. Allow to cool. Mix in shredded coconut, pecans, sour cream and fresh cream.

Put berry dip in centre of glass platter and arrange selected fruit, macaroons and marshmallows around bowl. Brush apple, pear and banana pieces slightly with strained lemon juice. Chill.

Serves 8–10

Pears with Chocolate Sauce

TRADITIONAL AND EVERYDAY DESSERTS

Wind the clock back to those Sunday lunches which finished with a steaming pudding or golden coloured crumble. This chapter brings all those favourite recipes back into the limelight with suggested variations and easy-to-follow instructions.

Sicilian Cassata

Gooseberry Bread Pudding

4 cups gooseberries
1½ cups sugar
½ cup water
1½ cups fresh white
*   breadcrumbs*
40 g butter
¼ teaspoon salt
3 eggs, separated
2 tablespoons icing sugar

Cook gooseberries in sugar and water for 15–20 minutes until tender. Add breadcrumbs, butter, salt and egg yolks. Beat 1 egg white until stiff and fold into pudding. Pour into greased baking dish and bake at 180°C (350°F) for 20 minutes.

To make meringue, beat remaining two egg whites until peaks form, fold in icing sugar and beat until stiff. Pile meringue on top of pudding and return to oven for further 10–15 minutes until top is light brown.

Serves 6

Pear and Date Crunch

750 g pears, peeled and
*   cored*
250 g dates, halved and
*   stoned*
1 tablespoon raw sugar
½ teaspoon ground allspice
½ cup orange juice

Topping

125 g butter
1¼ cups wholemeal flour
¼ cup raw or brown sugar
½ cup rolled oats
½ teaspoon cinnamon
pinch salt

Cut pears into chunky pieces and place in an ovenproof dish with dates, sugar, allspice and orange juice.

Rub butter into flour, stir in sugar, oats, cinnamon and salt. Sprinkle over fruit. Bake at 180°C (350°F) for 40 minutes until pears are soft and topping golden. Serve hot with yoghurt.

Serves 6

Pineapple Calypso

1 ripe pineapple
6 tablespoons chopped fresh
*   mint*
2 egg whites
½ cup caster sugar

Peel pineapple and cut into quarters lengthwise. Remove hard core from centre of each quarter and cut pineapple into small cubes. Mix with mint and leave in refrigerator overnight.

Spoon pineapple into serving bowl. Beat egg whites until stiff, add half the sugar, beating until dissolved. Beat in remaining sugar until dissolved. Spoon meringue over pineapple and place under griller to brown.

Apple and Plum Crumble

This easy dish works well with other fruits, too, such as apricots or peaches, in season.

500 g cooking apples
500 g plums
1 cup caster sugar
¼ cup orange juice
125 g butter
2¼ cups flour
grated rind 1 orange
½ cup flaked almonds

Preheat oven to 190°C (375°F).

Peel, core and slice apples. Halve and stone plums. Place half the fruit in a large, preferably clear, ovenproof dish. Sprinkle over ⅜ cup sugar and orange juice before placing remaining fruit in dish.

Rub together butter and flour until mixture resembles fine breadcrumbs. Stir in remaining sugar, orange rind and flaked almonds.

Sprinkle crumble mixture thickly over fruit and bake for 35–40 minutes or until top is slightly golden. Serve immediately, with whipped cream or custard.

Serves 6–8

Dried Fruit Crumble

1 cup dried apricots
1 cup dried figs
1 cup pitted prunes
¼ cup raisins
¼ cup currants
¼ cup sugar
1 cup water
¼ cup almonds
2 tablespoons flour
¼ cup desiccated coconut
¼ cup brown sugar
40 g butter

Soak fruit in enough water to cover for 1 hour. Drain. Place sugar and water in saucepan and bring to the boil. Add fruit and simmer for 30 minutes or until liquid has been absorbed. Add almonds and place mixture in ovenproof serving dish.

Combine all remaining ingredients and sprinkle over fruit. Bake at 200°C (400°F) for 15–20 minutes or until top is golden.

Serves 4

Apple and Plum Crumble

Wine Trifle

A popular British dessert which only improves if prepared a couple of days ahead.

1 sponge, cooked in Swiss
    roll tin
½ cup wine, sherry or port
4 bananas, sliced and
    sprinkled with lemon juice
1 packet lemon or port wine
    jelly

Custard

2 eggs
½ cup sugar
300 mL milk
1 teaspoon vanilla
2 teaspoons gelatine
1 tablespoon water

Garnish

whipped cream
toasted chopped almonds
maraschino cherries
    (optional)

Cut sponge into fingers, brush with wine, place around sides of spring form pan. Cut remaining sponge into triangles, place around base of tin, sprinkle with remaining wine. Arrange some of the banana on base.

Make jelly, allow to partly set then pour a small amount over sponge and fruit base. Set in refrigerator. Combine remaining jelly and banana, pour over base. Set in refrigerator.

To make custard, beat eggs and sugar, place in double boiler with milk, vanilla and gelatine softened in water. Cook, stirring until thick, cool, then pour over jelly and allow to set until firm.

Unmould carefully, tie with narrow ribbon. Decorate with whipped cream, almonds and cherries.

Serves 4–8

Rice Pudding

Rice pudding is not a name that conjures up visions of exotic culinary delights, but it is easy, cheap and nutritious — it can also be delicious and impressive. A basic rice pudding can be varied in many ways. Try adding beaten egg, spices such as cinnamon, raisins or chopped candied fruits or cream. Serve it with tropical fruits such as mango, pawpaw or passionfruit.

¼ cup short grain rice
40 g butter
2 tablespoons caster sugar
2½ cups milk
pinch grated nutmeg

Preheat oven to 150°C (300°F). Wash rice in a colander under running water and drain. Grease an ovenproof dish with some of the butter. Place rice and sugar in dish. Pour in milk and top with rest of butter, cut in small pieces. Dust with freshly grated nutmeg.

Bake for 2 hours, stirring pudding after ½ hour. Serve hot or cold.

Serves 4–6

Bread and Butter Pudding

5 eggs
4 tablespoons sugar
1 litre milk, warmed
1 teaspoon vanilla essence
3 tablespoons raisins
3–4 slices white bread,
    buttered

Topping

caster sugar
ground cinnamon

Preheat oven to 190°C (375°F).

Whisk eggs and sugar together until frothy. Add warmed milk and vanilla essence and pour into ovenproof dish. Add raisins. Cover top of custard with buttered bread, which may absorb mixture and sink.

Sprinkle sugar and cinnamon over pudding when bread forms a crust. Bake until custard has set.

Serves 4

Chocolate Marble Pudding

150 g self-raising flour
pinch salt
100 g butter
100 g caster sugar
2 eggs, beaten
a little milk
grated rind 1 lemon
few drops vanilla essence
2 tablespoons cocoa powder
butter for greasing

Sift together flour and salt. Place butter and sugar in a mixing bowl, food processor or blender and cream until light and fluffy.

Add beaten eggs gradually, beating all the time, then fold in sifted flour, ½ at a time. Stir in a little milk so that mixture is not too stiff.

Divide mixture between 2 bowls and add lemon rind and vanilla essence to one and cocoa to the other.

Grease a 1 litre pudding basin and add lemon and chocolate mixtures alternately, a spoonful at a time.

Cover securely with greased greaseproof paper, or aluminium foil, tie with string and steam for 1½–2 hours. Serve pudding very hot with chocolate sauce.

Note: You can use other flavourings and colourings to make a marble pudding. Try adding coffee essence, grated orange rind and juice or even cochineal to achieve different effects and flavours. Always add the different coloured mixtures in spoonfuls to get an attractive marbled effect.

Serves 6

Chocolate Marble Pudding

Spicy Apple Pie

1-1½ kg cooking apples
butter for greasing
½ teaspoon cinnamon
½ cup brown sugar
4 cloves
grated rind and juice 1
    lemon
3 tablespoons water
sweet shortcrust pastry made
    with 2 cups flour
2 teaspoons milk
2 tablespoons caster sugar

Preheat oven to 200°C (400°F). Peel, core and thinly slice apples. Butter a deep pie dish and arrange apples in layers with cinnamon and sugar. Spike some apple slices with cloves and sprinkle grated lemon rind and juice over top. Add water.

Roll out dough to diameter of pie dish and cover the pie. Trim edge, seal firmly, crimp and decorate. Make a small incision in top of pie.

Brush with milk and sprinkle with sugar. Bake in oven, reducing temperature to 180°C (350°F) after 10 minutes. Bake for another 20 minutes until pie is cooked and golden brown. Serve hot or cold with cream.

Serves 6

Queen of Puddings

2½ cups milk
¾ cup caster sugar
4 cups cake crumbs
grated rind 2 lemons
2 eggs, separated
¾ cup apricot jam

Preheat oven to 180°C (350°F). Heat milk and ¼ cup of sugar gently in a pan. Stir in cake crumbs and lemon rind, then remove from heat. Beat in egg yolks.

Pour half the mixture into a greased earthenware dish and bake for 30 minutes or until set.

Heat apricot jam in a saucepan and spread half over top of set custard. Top up dish with remaining egg yolk mixture and return to oven for 30 minutes or until set.

Cover top of pudding with rest of jam. Whisk egg whites with ⅓ cup of remaining sugar until stiff.

Raise oven temperature to 190°C (375°F). Pile whisked meringue on pudding and sprinkle with remaining sugar. Return to oven and bake for 5 minutes or until meringue is golden. Serve immediately.

Serves 6

Spotted Dick

1½ cups fresh breadcrumbs
75 g shredded suet
¼ cup caster sugar
⅔ cup currants, raisins or
    sultanas
¾ cup self-raising flour
pinch salt
⅓ cup milk
pinch cinnamon, ginger or
    nutmeg (optional)

Place breadcrumbs, shredded suet, sugar and currants in a bowl. Sift in flour and salt and mix well. Make a well in the mixture and mix in milk, a little at a time, until you have a soft dough. Add more milk if needed.

Grease a 1 litre mould (or basin) — use a fluted one for a more attractive appearance. Spoon mixture into mould or basin and cover loosely with two thicknesses of greaseproof paper, or aluminium foil. Tie with string and make sure it is well-sealed.

Steam over boiling water for 1½–2 hours. Turn out mould and serve with hot custard or a fruit sauce (see recipes).

Serves 4–6

Apricot Crisp

750 g apricots, halved and
    stoned
1¼ cups flour
1¼ cups brown sugar
pinch ground cloves
1 teaspoon cinnamon
185 g butter

Arrange apricots in greased, shallow ovenproof dish. Mix flour, sugar, cloves and cinnamon and rub in butter until mixture resembles coarse breadcrumbs. Sprinkle mixture evenly over apricots and pack down well. Bake at 190°C (375°F) for 30–40 minutes until crust is pale brown.

Serves 6

Cherry Jane

3 cups cherries, stoned
grated rind and juice ½
    lemon
2½ cups stale cake crumbs
2 tablespoons melted butter
1 cup sugar

Mix cherries with lemon rind and juice. Mix half the cake crumbs with melted butter. Grease a pie plate and cover base with a layer of cherries. Sprinkle with sugar and top with unbuttered crumbs. Repeat layers, topping finally with the buttered crumbs. Cover and bake at 180°C (350°F) for 45 minutes. Remove cover and bake further 15 minutes.

Serves 4

Honey Glazed Bananas

6 bananas, peeled
1/3 cup lemon juice
60 g butter
1/4 cup honey

Paint bananas with lemon juice. Melt butter, stir in honey and cook bananas over low heat, turning gently, until hot and glazed.

Serves 6

Glace Grapefruit

Glace Grapefruit

2 large grapefruit, halved
1 orange
1/2 cup caster sugar
4 tablespoons medium
   sherry
extra orange and grapefruit
   segments and shredded
   peel for garnish

Garnish

4 strawberries
mint leaves

Finely grate orange rind. Segment grapefruit and orange and dice. Reserve grapefruit halves. Blend flesh with sugar, sherry and rind. Fill grapefruit halves with mixture and freeze until set. Garnish with orange and grapefruit segments, shredded peel, mint leaves and halved strawberries.

Serves 4

1. Dice grapefruit and orange segments

2. Blend sugar with fruit, sherry and rind

3. Spoon mixture into grapefruit halves and freeze

Chocolate Cream Ice

A chocolate cream ice is usually flavoured with vanilla, unless rum or brandy is added.

2½ tablespoons sugar
⅓ cup water
3 egg yolks, well beaten
vanilla essence, or rum or
    brandy (optional)
200 g plain block chocolate
3 cups cream

Put sugar and water into a pan, dissolve sugar over gentle heat, then boil steadily until the syrup reaches the 'thread' stage. Have the well-beaten yolks ready. Carefully pour syrup on to them, whisk to a thick mousse-like mixture, add flavouring, then set aside.

Break up the chocolate, put into a pan with the cream and dissolve slowly over gentle heat. Bring it to scalding point, draw pan aside and allow to cool, then add to mousse. Chill mixture before freezing.

Serves 4–6

Sicilian Cassata

Although time consuming to prepare, this is a spectacular dessert to present at the dinner table. This is a homely and delicious version of this most famous Sicilian sweet.

700 g fresh ricotta
¾ cup sugar
4 (or more) tablespoons rum
1 cup candied lemon peel

100 g cooking chocolate
400 g sponge cake or sponge
    fingers

Using a large bowl and a wooden spoon, cream the ricotta until very smooth, add the sugar, 1 tablespoon rum, the candied peel and the chocolate chopped in very small pieces.

Sprinkle the remaining rum on the sponge cake (or sponge fingers) and line the bottom and sides of a mould or souffle dish.

Fill the mould with the ricotta mixture and refrigerate for at least three hours before serving. If you wish to unmould the cassata, line the mould with greaseproof paper brushed with rum.

Serves 6

Chocolate Almond Cream Flan

175 g margarine
75 g icing sugar
25 g cocoa powder
1 egg, beaten
275 g flour
30 g grated chocolate or
    caraque (see recipe)

Almond Cream

1¼ cups milk
¼ cup ground almonds
¼ cup caster sugar
⅓ cup cream
3 tablespoons cornflour

Preheat oven to 190°C (375°F).

Cream margarine and sugar together. Beat in cocoa and egg. Blend in flour gradually and knead to a smooth dough. Leave for 30 minutes.

Lightly grease a 20 cm fluted flan tin. Roll out pastry to 5 mm thick and line tin. Prick pastry base. Bake blind for 25 minutes. Allow to cool.

Meanwhile, bring milk to the boil. Remove from heat. Stir in ground almonds, sugar, cream and cornflour to make smooth, thick mixture. Heat gently, stirring, for 3–4 minutes, until well thickened. Allow to cool and pour into flan case. Chill until set. Sprinkle with grated chocolate or caraque, decorate with toffee almonds (see note), and serve.

Note: to make toffee almonds, put ½ cup sugar in small sauce-pan. Add 2–3 tablespoons water, dissolve and boil until mixture turns golden. Quickly drop almonds into it, coat them with toffee, lift out with teaspoon and drop on greased flat surface to set.

Serves 6

Chocolate Almond Cream Flan

1. Add candied peel and chocolate to the creamed ricotta

2. Line mould with sponge cake or fingers.

3. Fill mould with the ricotta mixture

Sweet Crepe Batter

Dessert crepes and pancakes are always popular, and avocados make them special. The batter recipe (below) is basic for all dessert crepes, and will make about 16 crepes.

1 cup flour
2 tablespoons raw sugar
1 egg, whole
1 egg yolk
1¼ cups milk
1 tablespoon melted butter

Sift flour into a bowl. Add sugar and make a well in the centre. Add the egg and yolk, beating with a wooden spoon until smooth. Gradually add combined milk and butter, beating well. Sieve then stand in refrigerator 1 hour before using.

Use a small amount of butter to grease a heavy frypan or crepe pan and allow pan to get fairly hot before pouring in batter.

For a crepe, don't pour too much mixture in. Tilt the pan as you do it to shape the crepe into a round. It is ready to turn when little bubbles appear on the surface.

Makes about 16

Note: Unfilled crepes or pancakes can be frozen. Allow to cool, one by one, before placing them in freezer. Frozen crepes will thaw out very quickly.

Orange Surprise

Smooth and creamy, this dessert is delicious served on a hot summer's evening. It can be prepared the day before and decorated just before serving. For variety, try it with lemons instead.

3 oranges, squeezed to make
 1 cup fresh orange juice
1 packet orange jelly crystals
¾ cup boiling water
2 cups natural yoghurt
½ cup cream
orange or lemon butterflies,
 for garnish

Cut oranges in halves, squeeze out juice and clean out pith so that orange skins can be used as serving dishes. Dissolve jelly in hot water and cool to room temperature. Stir in orange juice and then yoghurt until smooth. Refrigerate until mixture begins to set.

Remove from refrigerator and whip until mixture is foamy. Beat cream until fluffy and fold into mixture. Spoon into halved orange cups and refrigerate until set.

Serve garnished with orange or lemon butterflies on top with a little whipped cream.

Serves 4–6

Orange Surprise

MICROWAVING TRADITIONAL AND EVERYDAY DESSERTS

Apple Crumble

6 cooking apples, peeled and
    sliced
½ cup sugar
½ cup water
½ teaspoon cinnamon
60 g soft butter
¼ cup plain flour
½ cup brown sugar
½ cup coconut   TIME: 9 MINUTES

Place apples, water, sugar and cinnamon into a 1 litre casserole dish, cover and cook on HIGH 5 minutes. Rub butter into flour, coconut, brown sugar and sprinkle over apples. Top with extra cinnamon and cook on HIGH 3–4 minutes. Serve with Microwave Custard Sauce (see recipe).

Serves 6–8

Queen Pudding

4 slices of buttered, stale
    plain cake
5 eggs
2 tablespoons sugar
2 cups warm milk
vanilla
strawberry jam

Meringue

2 egg whites
5 tablespoons caster sugar
2 teaspoons cornflour   TIME: 6 MINUTES

Cut cake into cubes. Place into a well-buttered baking ring. Beat eggs, sugar and vanilla, add warm milk. Pour over cake cubes and cook 60 minutes on DEFROST.

Spread top of custard with strawberry jam. Whip egg whites until stiff, gradually adding sugar. Beat to dissolve. Fold in cornflour. Pipe onto custard and cook on HIGH 2–3 minutes.

Serves 6

Baked Bread and Butter Custard

30 g butter
2 cups milk
5 eggs
¼ cup raw sugar
1 teaspoon vanilla
4 slices white bread, crusts
    removed, then buttered
nutmeg
2 tablespoons sultanas   TIME: 1 HOUR

Place butter into milk and heat for 2 minutes. Beat eggs, sugar and vanilla, add milk and butter mixture. Sprinkle buttered bread lightly with nutmeg, cut into cubes, and place into a greased baking ring with sultanas. Pour custard over bread and cook uncovered 60 minutes on DEFROST.

Serves 6

Orange Sponge Pudding

40 g butter
2 tablespoons sugar
1 egg
¾ cup self-raising flour
¼ cup milk
1 tablespoon orange juice or
    Grand Marnier
1 tablespoon grated orange
    rind
Orange Sauce (see recipe)   TIME: 4–5 MINUTES

Cream butter and sugar; beat in egg. Fold in flour, milk, orange juice and rind. Lightly grease china pudding basin and place a small circle of greaseproof paper in the bottom. Top with sponge mixture and cook on HIGH 4–5 minutes. Turn out onto serving plate. Mask with Orange Sauce.

Serves 4–6

Orange Sauce

2 tablespoons sugar
1 tablespoon cornflour
⅔ cup strained orange juice
⅓ cup water
1 tablespoon Grand Marnier
40 g butter
1 tablespoon grated orange
    rind
2 teaspoons strained lemon
    juice   TIME: 2½ MINUTES

Blend sugar, cornflour and orange juice in jug and cook on HIGH 2–2½ minutes, stirring twice during cooking. Mix in remaining ingredients and serve warm over Orange Sponge Pudding (see recipe).

Makes about 1 cup

Strawberry Cheese Cake

1½ tablespoons butter
1¼ cups biscuit crumbs
500 g cream cheese, softened
½ cup caster sugar
2 egg yolks
1 teaspoon grated lemon
   rind
1 tablespoon lemon juice,
   strained
2 egg whites, stiffly beaten

Topping

1 cup sour cream
1 tablespoon sugar
1 teaspoon vanilla essence
1 punnet strawberries
½ cup apricot jam, to glaze   TIME: 23 MINUTES

Place butter in bowl and soften on HIGH 1 minute. Stir in biscuit crumbs and cook on HIGH 2 minutes. Press crumb mixture into base of flan dish.

In a large bowl beat cream cheese, sugar, egg yolks, rind and juice until creamy. Avoid overbeating. Fold in stiffly beaten egg whites, using a metal spoon. Pour into prepared dish and cook on DEFROST 20 minutes. Allow to cool.

In a small bowl beat sour cream, sugar and vanilla until sugar dissolves. Spread over cheese cake. Wash and dry strawberries, place upright on cheese cake.

Heat apricot jam, sieve and coat strawberries. Chill several hours before serving.

Serves 8–12

Microwave Custard Sauce

This basic sauce recipe can be served with fruit for a quick dessert or as an accompaniment for pies and puddings.

1½ cups milk
3 tablespoons sugar
2 tablespoons custard
   powder
2 egg yolks
1 teaspoon vanilla
¼ teaspoon cinnamon
1 tablespoon sugar   TIME: 6–7 MINUTES

Combine milk, sugar and custard powder in jug and cook on HIGH 4 minutes until sauce thickens, stirring after 2 minutes.

Beat egg yolks in basin and whisk. Blend in 2 tablespoons of custard mixture and whisk egg mixture into remaining custard. Cook on DEFROST 1–2 minutes. Blend in vanilla.

Combine cinnamon and sugar and sprinkle on surface of custard to prevent skin forming.

Makes about 4 cups

Meringue-Topped Chocolate Cheese Cake

Base

1 cup biscuit crumbs
½ cup melted margarine

Filling

375 g cream cheese, softened
2 eggs
½ cup caster sugar
1 teaspoon vanilla
60 g chocolate (to melt
   chocolate, cut up and
   place in oven and cook 1
   minute on HIGH)

Meringue

2 egg whites
5 tablespoons caster sugar
⅓ cup coconut
2 teaspoons cornflour   TIME: 9 MINUTES

Combine ingredients and press evenly in a 20 cm pyrex pie plate. Chill until firm.

Beat softened cream cheese using an electric mixer until smooth. Add eggs one at a time. Add sugar, vanilla, and beat until creamy smooth. Pour into crumb crust. Swirl in melted chocolate to give a marble effect. Cook on HIGH 3 minutes.

Whip egg whites until stiff, gradually adding sugar, beating to dissolve. Fold in coconut (can be lightly toasted if desired) and cornflour. Pipe onto cheese cake and cook on HIGH 3 minutes. Serve cold.

DEFROSTING DESSERTS
The microwave is ideal for preparing and cooking desserts. It can also be used to quickly defrost frozen cakes, crepes, or fruit for the evening's pudding. Simply unwrap the frozen dessert, place on a microwave-safe platter and DEFROST 1–4 minutes until a toothpick can be easily inserted into the centre of the dessert. Once defrosted, allow the dessert to stand 5–10 minutes before glazing, piping or decorating it.

Strawberry Cheese Cake

PIES, TARTS AND PASTRIES

The light, crispy texture of pastry creates a perfect foil for fruit, creamy fillings and fragrant custards. The versatility of these desserts means they can be dressed up or down to suit any occasion from an informal family lunch to the grandest of dinners.

Fruit Pizza

Fruit Pizza

2 cups self-raising flour
1 to 2 tablespoons sugar
½ teaspoon salt
30 g butter, cut into cubes
¾ cup milk

Topping

250 g cream cheese, softened
¼ cup caster sugar
1 teaspoon grated lemon
   rind
6 cups sliced fresh fruit
   (kiwifruit, strawberries,
   mango, peeled grapes
   etc.)
⅔ cup apple or orange juice
2 teaspoons arrowroot

Sift flour, sugar and salt into a bowl. Cut butter into small cubes and rub into flour. Add milk, blending mixture with a butter knife to form a soft dough. Turn dough onto a floured board and knead lightly. Cover and refrigerate for 10 minutes. Roll dough out into a 30 cm circle and place onto a lightly greased round ovenproof dish.

Bake at 220°C (425°F) for 12–15 minutes until well browned. Allow to cool. Place softened cream cheese in a bowl and beat in sugar until dissolved.

Add grated lemon rind and spread mixture evenly over pizza crust. Arrange sliced fruits on top.

Combine arrowroot with a little of the juice in a small bowl. Gradually add the remaining juice stirring until smooth. Heat in a small saucepan until boiling. Cook stirring constantly for 3 minutes or until thickened. Cool until lukewarm. Spoon over fruit and chill until set.

Serves 12

```
SUCCESSFUL PASTRY
☐ Handle the pastry as little as possible, using only the
  fingertips to rub the fat into the flour.
☐ Add just enough liquid to bind the dough. A dough
  which is too wet will be unmanageable and shrink dur-
  ing cooking, resulting in a tough pastry.
☐ When the pastry has been mixed, wrap it in plastic and
  leave it in the fridge for 20 minutes, this makes it easier
  to handle and stops it from shrinking during cooking.
☐ If, during rolling, the pastry becomes sticky and hard
  to manage, pop it into the freezer for 5 minutes and
  then start again.
```

Honey and Treacle Tart

1 quantity sweet shortcrust
   pastry (see recipe)
⅓ cup treacle
1 tablespoon honey
juice and grated rind 1
   lemon
2 cups cornflakes

Preheat oven to 220°C (425°F). Roll out pastry on lightly floured board to a thickness of 5 mm and line a 23 cm pie plate. Trim edges, reserving trimmings. Flute edges.

In a bowl, blend together treacle, honey, lemon juice and rind. Place cornflakes in a polythene bag and crush with a rolling pin. Mix thoroughly with treacle mixture.

Prick pastry with a fork. Spoon filling into pastry case and spread evenly. Roll out remaining pastry and cut into strips. Lay in a lattice pattern on top of tart, sealing edges as you go. Bake tart in oven for 15–20 minutes or until pastry is golden brown. Serve with a jug of creamy, hot custard, or cold whipped cream.

Serves 6

Mulberry Pie

Pastry

1½ cups flour
1½ cups self-raising flour
2 tablespoons caster sugar
250 g butter
1 egg yolk
2–4 tablespoons cold water

Filling

5 cups mulberries
½ cup water
1 cup sugar
3 tablespoons arrowroot
1 cup stewed apple, drained

To make pastry, sift flours and sugar together. Rub in butter until mixture resembles fine breadcrumbs. Mix in egg yolk and sufficient water to make a firm dough. Roll out half the pastry on lightly floured board and line 30 cm pie dish. Reserve remainder of pastry.

To make filling, cook mulberries with water and sugar for 15–20 minutes until soft. Strain through a coarse sieve, pushing gently with back of spoon. Discard seeds. Return puree to saucepan. Mix arrowroot to paste with small amount of water, add to puree and cook, stirring constantly until thickened. Add apple and allow to cool. Spoon into pastry-lined pie dish and cover with remaining pastry. Crimp edges to seal. Bake at 230°C (450°F) for 10–15 minutes until browned then reduce to 200°C (400°F) and continue cooking for further 15–20 minutes.

Serves 6–8

Pumpkin Pie

In the USA, pumpkin is often cooked as a dessert. Pumpkin Pie is well-loved by American cooks. This is the traditional Thanksgiving dessert — preceded by baked turkey of course.

Pastry

cup self-raising flour
cup wholemeal flour
25 g butter
egg yolk
tablespoons lemon juice
iced water

Filling

50 g cooked pumpkin
tablespoon brown sugar
eggs, separated
tablespoons cream
¼ teaspoon nutmeg
¼ teaspoon ground ginger

Place flours in bowl and rub in butter. Combine egg yolk with lemon juice, work into dough. Add enough iced water to form a firm dough. Wrap in plastic and refrigerate 20 minutes. Roll out to fit 20 cm pie plate and stand for 20 minutes in refrigerator.

Puree pumpkin with sugar, egg yolks, cream, nutmeg and ginger. Beat egg whites until stiff and fold into pumpkin. Pour mixture into pie plate and bake at 180°C (350°F) for 35 minutes or until pastry is golden and filling has set. Serve warm.

Serves 4-6

Wholemeal Shortcrust Pastry

1 cup flour
1 cup wholemeal flour
pinch salt
120 g butter cut into small
    cubes
¼ cup iced water
squeeze lemon juice

Sift the flours and salt together into a bowl. Return the husks to the flour. Using your fingertips, rub the butter into the flour lifting the flour high as you go so as to incorporate the maximum air. Continue until the mixture resembles breadcrumbs.

Make a well in the centre and add the liquid a little at a time, mixing with a rounded blade knife until the mixture forms a dough. If the dough seems dry and will not come together add a little extra liquid.

With the fingers of one hand knead the dough to form a smooth ball. Cover with plastic wrap and refrigerate for 30 minutes.

Uncover the dough, place onto a lightly floured board. Rub a rolling pin with a little flour and roll out the dough to the desired shape and thickness, line pie plate or flan tin then refrigerate for 15 minutes before baking to prevent shrinking.

Makes sufficient to line a 23–25 cm pie plate

Pumpkin Pie

Sweet Shortcrust Pastry

This recipe makes sufficient pastry to line a 20–23 cm pie plate or flan tin.

1½ cups flour
pinch salt
¼ teaspoon baking powder
2 tablespoons caster sugar
125 g chilled butter cut into
    small cubes
1 egg yolk
2 teaspoons chilled water
squeeze lemon juice

Sift flour, salt, baking powder and caster sugar into a bowl. Add the butter and rub into the flour using your fingertips until the mixture resembles fine breadcrumbs. Make a well in the centre and add the combined egg yolk, water and lemon juice mixing with a round bladed knife until the mixture forms a soft dough. Add extra liquid if necessary. Use the fingers of one hand to knead the dough lightly in the bowl and gather it together into a ball. Cover with plastic wrap and refrigerate for 30 minutes.

Uncover dough and place on a lightly floured board. Rub a rolling pin with a little flour and roll out the dough using short, firm strokes lifting and turning the dough frequently to make sure that it hasn't stuck.

Roll dough to required shape and thickness, line pie plate or flan tin then refrigerate again for 15 minutes before baking to prevent shrinking.

Baked Pear Surprise

These are not exactly pies, but fruit served hot in pastry jackets.

125 g butter
4 tablespoons sugar
⅛ teaspoon cinnamon
¼ cup ground almonds
1 egg, separated
1 tablespoon orange liqueur
4 eating pears, ripe and
    tender
500 g puff pastry (see recipe)
2 tablespoons apricot jam

Make a stiff paste by creaming butter, sugar, cinnamon and ground almonds together. Gradually add egg yolk. Stir in orange liqueur.

Peel and core pears. Split in half. Fill centres with paste and press the two halves together.

Roll out puff pastry into 4 oblongs, 20 cm x 10 cm. Place a pear in the middle of each. Brush edges with water and fold oblong to enclose each pear, retaining the conical shape. Make two small cuts at the top to allow steam to escape. Brush with egg white. Rest for 15 minutes.

Grease 2 baking trays. Place pears on them and bake at 200°C (400°F) for 20 minutes.

Heat apricot jam until liquid and strain. When pears are taken from oven, brush them lightly with hot jam as a glaze. Serve hot with ice cream or custard.

Serves 4

Note: Leave stalks on peeled pears for a very attractive effect. This recipe can be used with apples and peaches.

Plum Flan

Pastry

100 g butter
1⅓ cups wholemeal flour
1 egg yolk
a little milk

Filling

3 egg yolks
¼ cup honey
300 mL natural yoghurt
½ teaspoon powdered
   cinnamon
500 g small plums, halved
   and stoned
½ cup blanched almonds
1 tablespoon brown sugar

Rub butter into flour, add egg yolk and enough milk to form firm dough. Roll out and line 20 cm flan dish. Prick base a few times with fork.

Beat yolks with honey, yoghurt and cinnamon. Pour into pastry case.

Arrange plums, cut side down in yoghurt mixture. Bake at 200°C (400°F) for 35–40 minutes, until custard is set. Sprinkle with nuts and brown sugar and brown under a hot grill.

Serves 6

Apricot and Nut Flan

Pastry

1 cup flour
2 tablespoons chopped
   almonds
2 tablespoons chopped
   walnuts
1 tablespoon sugar
2 tablespoons butter
1 egg
2 tablespoons lemon juice
iced water

Filling

1 x 425 g can apricot halves
2 tablespoons chopped dried
   apricots
4 tablespoons chopped
   almonds
1 egg yolk
2 egg whites
4 tablespoons sugar
extra apricot halves for
   decoration if desired

Place flour, nuts and sugar in a bowl and rub in butter. Combine egg and lemon juice, add to dough. Add enough iced water to form a firm dough. Wrap in plastic and allow to stand 20 minutes in refrigerator. Roll out to fit 18 cm flan tin. Refrigerate while preparing filling.

Drain apricots and puree in blender or strain through sieve. Mix in dried apricots, almonds and egg yolk. Beat egg whites until stiff, beat in sugar until dissolved. Fold into apricot mixture. Spoon mixture into flan and bake at 180°C (350°F) for 1 hour. For a party, decorate with additional apricot halves.

Serves 4–6

Fruity Flan

2 cups pastry cream (see
   recipe)

Pastry

2 cups biscuit crumbs
½ cup ground hazelnuts
1 teaspoon grated orange
   rind
¾–1 cup melted butter

Topping (illustrated)

½ honeydew melon scooped
   into balls
½ rock melon, scooped into
   balls
300 g muscat grapes
½ kiwano (hornmelon)
2 guavas, sliced
1 strawberry
or use selected fruit in season
   — grapes, strawberries,
   kiwifruit, peaches,
   apricots

Glaze

½ cup apricot jam
1 tablespoon orange liqueur
   or juice

Prepare pastry cream day before and store in refrigerator until needed.

Combine dry pastry ingredients with butter. Press mixture around base and sides of a 25 cm flan tin and bake at 180°C (350°F) 10 minutes. Cool.

Pour pastry cream into prepared pastry case and allow to set. Arrange fruit pieces attractively over filling.

Warm apricot jam gently, stir in liqueur, sieve then quickly brush hot glaze over fruit and allow to set.

Serve Fruity Flan well chilled.

Serves 6–8

Cream Cheese Pockets

With just a few ingredients in the cupboard you can make this quick and tasty dessert.

3 tablespoons currants
4 tablespoons sweet sherry
2 glace apricots
2 tablespoons chopped glace
    ginger
3 tablespoons chopped
    hazelnuts
2 tablespoons sugar
2 cups ricotta cheese
1 teaspoon mixed spice
8 sheets filo pastry
125 g unsalted butter,
    melted

Simmer currants in sherry for 10 minutes. Chop apricots and place in bowl with ginger, hazelnuts, sugar, cheese and mixed spice. Stir in currants.

Cut filo pastry into halves across sheets. Brush each sheet with melted butter. Place 1 tablespoon of mixture on each sheet and fold up into a square parcel. Place squares on oiled baking tray and bake at 200°C (400°F) for 10 minutes.

Serves 4–6

Zabaglione Cream Squares with Avocado

Zabaglione is a widely loved Italian dessert. The addition of avocado transforms these pastry squares into something superb.

250 g puff pastry (see recipe)
2 avocados, very thinly sliced

Zabaglione Cream

3 egg yolks
2 tablespoons raw sugar
3 tablespoons Marsala wine
1 cup stiffly whipped cream

Roll pastry out to a 23 cm square. Cut into 9 squares. Bake on a greased tray at 200°C (400°F) for 10 minutes or until lightly browned. Cool on a wire rack.

Whisk the egg, sugar and Marsala together in a double boiler or heatproof bowl over simmering water. Continue whisking until mixture becomes frothy and thick and rises. Cool.

Fold in the whipped cream. Refrigerate for 1 hour before using.

To serve, carefully cut each square of pastry in half. Pipe or spread the Zabaglione Cream into the bottom square and decorate with thinly sliced avocado. Replace pastry top. Finely chopped roasted almonds or hazelnuts can be sprinkled over the avocado before replacing the lid.

Serves 9

Note: Fruit juice can be substituted for the Marsala wine.

Lemon Tart

½ quantity orange crust
    pastry (see recipe)
6 eggs
⅔ cup sugar
juice 4 lemons
1½ cups cream
125 g butter, melted
1 lemon, sliced, for garnish

Roll out pastry on lightly floured board and line a 25 cm loose bottom flan tin. Cover pastry with foil, and place dried beans or uncooked rice on foil and bake at 200°C (400°F) for 5 minutes. Remove foil and beans and bake further 5 minutes. Allow to cool.

Beat eggs and sugar until light and lemon coloured. Stir in lemon juice, cream and butter. Pour into pastry case and bake at 160°C (325°F) for 45 minutes until firm. Spread with extra whipped cream and garnish with slices of lemon.

Serves 6

Orange Crust Pastry

2½ cups flour
½ teaspoon salt
½ cup cold unsalted butter
½ cup cold margarine
1 teaspoon grated orange
    rind
4 tablespoons cold orange
    juice

Sift flour with salt. Cut in butter and margarine; add orange rind. Rub with fingertips until the texture resembles coarse crumbs.

Using a knife, cut orange juice into flour mixture to form a soft dough. (Do not overwork.) Refrigerate 1 hour before using.

Makes enough for 2 × 22 cm or 25 cm open tarts, or 1 × 23 cm or 25 cm pie with lid.

FREEZING PIES AND TARTS
Unbaked pies and tarts can be frozen successfully unless they have cooked custard fillings or are topped with meringue or cream. The best procedure is to open freeze pies and tarts on a foil-lined baking tray until solid. Cover with foil and seal in freezer bag. They will keep about 3 months. Thaw at room temperature or defrost in a microwave oven before baking and decorating.

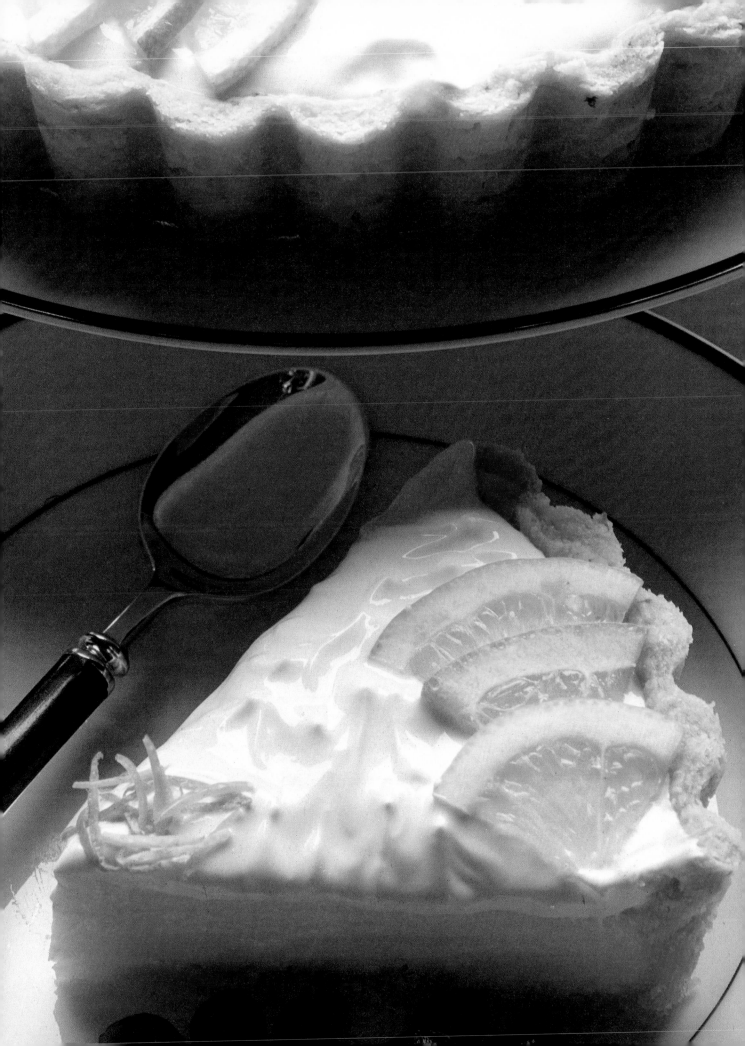

Creamed Avocado Puffs

Everyone loves cream puffs, and with avocado filling they simply melt in the mouth.

Puff Mixture

1 cup water
70 g butter, cut in small
  pieces
1 tablespoon raw sugar
1 cup flour, sifted
4 eggs

Filling

⅔ cup raw sugar
1 teaspoon vanilla essence
5 egg yolks
⅔ cup flour
1½ cups milk
2 cups chopped avocado
a little Creme de Menthe
  may be added
1 cup whipped cream
  sweetened with a little
  honey

Garnish

1 avocado, finely sliced
16 strawberries, finely sliced
icing sugar

Place water, butter and sugar in pan and stir to completely melt butter. Bring to boil and remove from heat. Add flour all at once and stir vigorously. Reheat mixture for 2 minutes until the dough forms a ball.

Remove from heat and beat eggs well into mixture, one at a time. Butter and flour oven trays and, using 2 spoons, form balls about the size of an egg. Place 8 cm apart on tray.

Bake at 200°C (400°F) for 20 minutes or until puffed and golden brown.

Beat sugar, vanilla essence and yolks until thick and lemon coloured. Beat in flour. Heat milk and add to egg, sugar and flour mixture. Cook over moderate heat, stirring, to form a thick custard. Cool.

Mix the chopped avocado with the Creme de Menthe and whipped cream.

Slice top off each puff. Fill with cooled custard and remaining space with avocado cream. Garnish with avocado slices and finely sliced strawberries. Replace cream puff lid. Dust with sifted icing sugar before serving.

Serves 8

Custard and Avocado Tart

A tart with a rich pastry that can be served slightly warm or chilled.

Pastry

60 g butter
125 g plain flour
2 egg yolks
1 whole egg
30 g raw sugar

Filling

1 cup milk
1 cup cream
125 g raw sugar or honey
2 teaspoons vanilla essence
4 eggs, separated
1 large avocado (or 2
  medium-sized)

Cut butter into flour and mix with fingertips until it develops a sandy texture. Mix egg yolks and egg with sugar and combine with flour mix. Form into a ball and refrigerate 30 minutes before using.

Grease a 20 cm pie dish and press pastry evenly in with fingertips over the bottom and sides. (This pastry has a very crumbly consistency and cannot be rolled.)

Prick all over with a fork and bake at 200°C (400°F) for only 5 minutes.

Blend all of the filling ingredients (except for egg whites) until smooth.

Beat egg whites separately until soft peaks form; fold gently into custard with a metal spoon.

Pour in filling and bake at 180°C (350°F) for 20 to 30 minutes or until set.

Serve at room temperature with whipped cream or serve cold.

Serves 6–8

Note: The cream can be sprinkled with a little ground cinnamon or nutmeg after garnishing the tart; alternatively, decorate by dusting icing sugar over a doily placed on the tart.

AVOCADO DESSERTS

There are a few little hints about preparing avocado desserts that make a big difference. Once cut, avocado loses its colour and browns easily. Keep this in mind when preparing uncooked avocado desserts or fillings — they will usually keep well in the refrigerator for up to 2 days.

To retain the subtle flavour of avocados in cooked puddings such as Custard and Avocado Tart, make sure that you don't overcook. Avocados sometimes develop a bitter flavour if cooked too long.

Custard and Avocado Tart

Cherry Shortcake

Fresh Fig Shortcake

1 quantity short pastry (see
  Cherry Shortcake recipe)
500 g fresh figs
1 × 250 g jar raspberry jam
2½ tablespoons sugar
2 tablespoons maraschino
1 egg, beaten

Line a baking dish with the pastry. Peel the figs and macerate them for about 30 minutes in the maraschino and sugar.

Spread the raspberry jam on the bottom of the pastry and cover with the figs.

Using a pastry wheel, cut the leftover pastry into long ribbons. Arrange the pastry ribbons into a lattice. Brush the pastry with the beaten egg. Bake in a pre-heated oven at 180°C (350°F) for 45 minutes. Serve hot or cold.

Cherry Shortcake

Pastry	Filling
2⅓ cups flour	1 × 250 g jar cherry jam
pinch of salt	800 g dark red cherries,
⅔ cup sugar	stoned
grated peel of 1 lemon	2 tablespoons icing sugar
2 eggs	
150 g butter	

To prepare the pastry, sift flour onto a board, add salt, sugar and the grated lemon peel, mix together and make a well in the centre. Break in 1 egg and add the butter cut in pieces. Knead with the fingertips, taking care not to work the pastry too much. When smooth, shape into a ball, roll in buttered greaseproof paper and refrigerate for 30 minutes.

Roll the pastry out to a thickness of 5 mm and line a tart or quiche dish which you have previously buttered and floured. Using a pastry wheel, cut the leftover pastry into long ribbons.

Spread the cherry jam on the bottom of the pastry and cover with the washed and stoned cherries. Sprinkle with the icing sugar and arrange the pastry ribbons into a lattice. Brush the pastry with the remaining beaten egg. Bake in a pre-heated oven at 180°C (350°F) for 45 minutes. Serve hot or cold.

Serves 6

Strawberry Flan

sweet shortcrust pastry made
  with 2 cups flour
1½ cups pastry cream (see
  recipe)

punnet strawberries, hulled
½ cup redcurrant jelly, to
  glaze
toasted almond slivers, to
  garnish

Roll out pastry to fit a 24 cm flan case and form high fluted border. Crush greaseproof paper and place into pastry case. Leave in refrigerator 10 minutes if pastry is soft.

Place 1½ cups dried beans or rice on greaseproof paperlining and bake blind in oven 180°C (350°F) for 15 minutes. Remove beans and paper, bake further 5 minutes. Pastry should not be coloured.

When cool, remove flan case from ring and fill with pastry cream. Cover with halved strawberries. Warm redcurrant jelly to liquid and spoon over strawberries. Sprinkle with almond slivers to serve.

Serves 6

1. Shape pastry dough into a ball

2. Line a tart or quiche dish

3. Spread pastry with cherry jam and cover with stoned cherries

Festive Fruit Tarts

Festive fruit tarts are easy to make — just fill them with your favourite fruits and garnish with almonds and cherries.

sweet shortcrust pastry made
    with 1½ cups flour
1 × 225 g jar apricot jam
1 tablespoon orange juice
7 mandarin segments
10 strawberries
1 cup flaked almonds
1 green glace cherry

2 apricots
1 tablespoon pistachio nuts
⅓ cup canned redcurrants
1 banana, sliced

Preheat the oven to 200°C (400°F). On a floured board, roll out the pastry to 0.5 cm thick. Lightly grease and flour 6 patty or tartlet tins and line them with pastry. Prick with a fork and bake blind for 20 minutes.

To prepare the apricot glaze melt the apricot jam and orange juice in a saucepan then push through a fine sieve.

To fill the tarts as shown in the picture, clockwise from top left: arrange 7 mandarin segments in the first. Cover with apricot glaze. In the second, arrange 5 strawberries, interspersed with flaked almonds, and put a green glace cherry in the middle. Glaze lightly.

Cut an apricot in half; remove the stone. Put a strawberry in one half and arrange slices of the other half around it. Alternate the slices with pistachio nuts, and glaze. Fill the fourth tart with redcurrants and stud it with almond flakes. Glaze lightly.

Cut the rest of the strawberries in half and arrange them in a rosette in the fifth tart. Centre with half a strawberry on a slice of banana. Glaze. Fill the sixth tart with banana slices garnished with redcurrants and pistachio nuts. Glaze. Serve on a dish garnished with the other apricot, halved and filled with redcurrants.

Makes 6

Passionfruit Avocado and Yoghurt Flan

A highly nutritious dish that keeps well.

Pastry

1⅔ cups plain flour
½ cup desiccated coconut
1 tablespoon sugar
125 g soft butter
apple juice or water to
    moisten

Filling

3 eggs
5 tablespoons honey
1 teaspoon vanilla
1½ cups natural yoghurt
4 large passionfruit
2 large avocados, mashed

Mix flour, coconut and sugar. Cut in butter with long-bladed knife and rub with fingertips until it resembles breadcrumbs. Add enough apple juice or water to make dough come together.

Form a ball, wrap in plastic and refrigerate for at least 1 hour before using.

Roll out pastry and line a 23 cm pie dish.

Beat eggs, honey, vanilla and yoghurt. Mix mashed avocados and passionfruit pulp into egg mix.

Pour into prepared pastry case and bake at 180°C (350°F) for about 30 minutes until just set.

Cool and serve with whipped cream, extra passionfruit sprinkled with cinnamon, or nutmeg.

Serves 8–10

Festive Fruit Tarts

Fruit Turnovers

500 g puff pastry (see recipe)
1 egg, beaten

Apple Filling

⅓ cup sultanas
1 tablespoon rum
1 tablespoon butter
375 g cooking apples,
  peeled, cored and sliced
¼ cup water
⅓ cup sugar
pinch ground mixed spices
  or cloves

Prune Filling

1½ cups dried prunes
150 mL tepid water
⅓ cup sugar
rind 1 lemon, cut into strips
½ cup red wine
pinch cinnamon

Preheat oven to 200°C (400°F). Roll out pastry to about 2 mm thick. Cut 8 rounds with a 15 cm pastry cutter and roll them into ovals.

Soak sultanas in rum. Meanwhile melt butter in a saucepan. Add apple, cover and simmer for 4 minutes. Pour in water and simmer for 10 minutes until apples are soft. Stir in sugar and spice and cook for another minute. Remove from heat and stir in soaked sultanas.

To make the alternative prune filling, soak prunes in tepid water for 2 hours in pan. Then add sugar, lemon rind, wine and cinnamon, and cook for 20 minutes. Cool, drain, and remove stones.

Divide filling between each oval. Brush edges with water. Fold pastry over and press edges together. Brush the tops of turnovers with egg and score a lattice pattern lightly with the back of a knife. Bake for 20 minutes or until turnovers are golden brown. Serve hot or cold.

Makes 8

Crostoli (Sweet Fritters)

These are the traditional Italian Lenten sweet, when all flour, sugar and oil should be used up before forty days of fasting. The English and Irish pancakes have, of course, the same origin.

3 cups flour
50 g butter
1 tablespoon sugar
2 eggs
1 teaspoon vanilla essence
pinch salt
oil for deep frying (peanut or
  sunflower)
icing sugar

Combine the flour, butter, sugar, eggs, vanilla and pinch of salt and knead into a smooth soft dough. Shape it into a ball, cover it with a kitchen towel and let it rest for an hour or so.

With a rolling pin, roll the dough out very thinly (the thickness of a 20 cent piece). Cut into ribbons and twist in bows, butterflies, or whatever shape takes your fancy.

Heat enough oil for deep frying and drop the crostoli in a few at a time until golden and a little puffed. Drain on paper towel, sprinkle with icing sugar and serve hot or cold.

Serves 4

CROSTOLI
Crostoli are sweet Italian fritters. For the best results, dust with icing sugar just before serving. Icing sugar is readily absorbed into the cooked fritters, particularly if they are still hot.

Crostoli

1. Roll the dough out very thinly

2. Cut rolled dough into ribbons or twist into bows

3. Deep fry crostoli until puffed and golden

Caramel Tart

Pastry

125 g butter
1/3 cup sugar
2 cups flour, sifted
3 drops vanilla
2 teaspoons water
1 egg yolk

Filling

2 tablespoons butter
1 cup brown sugar
4 egg yolks
3 drops vanilla
pinch salt
2 tablespoons flour
2 cups milk

Meringue

3 egg whites
1/2 cup caster sugar

TIME: 8 MINUTES

Rub butter into sugar and flour. Add vanilla, water and egg yolk. Knead lightly and let rest 15 minutes. Roll out pastry and line a 23 cm pie plate. Prick well and cook on HIGH for 4 minutes. Allow to cool.

Beat butter and sugar until fluffy. Beat in egg yolks. Add vanilla, salt, fold in sifted flour, stir in milk. Cook 4–5 minutes, stirring every minute until mixture thickens. Spoon into pastry case. Top with meringue and cook 2–3 minutes on HIGH.

Beat egg whites, adding sugar, 1 tablespoon at a time, until soft peaks form. Pipe or spread over filling and cook to set for 2–3 minutes. Place under grill for a few minutes if a light golden colour is required.

Serves 6–8

Lemon Meringue Pie

Filling

1/2 cup cornflour
1/2 cup sugar
3/4 cup water
1/3 cup lemon juice
1/3 cup butter
3 egg yolks
grated rind of 1 lemon

1 × 20 cm precooked pastry case

Meringue

3 egg whites
1/2 cup caster sugar

TIME: 8 MINUTES

Combine cornflour, sugar, water, juice of lemon and butter in a casserole dish and cook on HIGH 2 minutes, stir and cook a further 2 minutes. Cool. Beat in yolks and lemon rind. Place in pastry case.

Beat egg whites adding sugar 1 tablespoon at a time. Pipe or spread over filling and cook on HIGH 2–3 minutes. Place under grill for a few minutes if a light golden colour is required. Cool.

Serves 6

Cinnamon Pear Upside Down Tart

This tart is equally delicious cooked with apples.

4 firm pears, halved, peeled
  and cored
1/2 cup sugar
1/2 teaspoon cinnamon
2 1/2 cups red wine

Dough

250 g butter
4 cups flour, sifted
2 teaspoons salt
3–4 tablespoons iced water

TIME: 35 MINUTES

Rub butter into flour and salt. Cut water through to form a soft dough. Knead lightly on floured board. Wrap in plastic wrap and refrigerate.

Arrange pear halves, cut-side up, in a 30 cm baking dish. Sprinkle over sugar and cinnamon. Pour over red wine to cover. Cover and cook on HIGH 5 minutes, then reduce to MEDIUM and cook 10 minutes. Drain liquid into jug. Cook on HIGH 10 minutes.

Pour sauce over pears. Roll out dough, cover dish, seal and trim edges. Cook on MEDIUM high 10 minutes. Cool 5 minutes then unmould on serving plate. Serve with whipped cream.

Serves 4–6

Cinnamon Pear Upside Down Tart

Pineapple Meringue Pie

Pastry

125 g butter
1/3 cup sugar
2 cups flour, sifted
3 drops vanilla
2 teaspoons water
1 egg yolk

Filling

1 × 500 g can pineapple,
  crushed
1 egg yolk
2 tablespoons custard
  powder
1 tablespoon arrowroot
1/4 cup orange juice

Meringue

3 egg whites
1/2 cup caster sugar

TIME: 13 MINUTES

Rub butter into sugar and flour. Add vanilla, water and egg yolk. Knead lightly and let rest 15 minutes. Roll out pastry and line a 23 cm pie plate. Prick well and cook for 4 minutes. Allow to cool.

Place pineapple into a casserole dish and cook on HIGH 4 minutes until boiling. Beat egg yolk, add custard powder, arrowroot and orange juice. Mix into hot pineapple and cook for 2 minutes. Cool and spoon into pastry case.

Beat egg whites, adding sugar, 1 tablespoon at a time, until soft peaks form. Pipe or spread over pineapple filling and cook to set for 2–3 minutes. Place under grill for a few minutes if a light golden colour is required.

Serves 6–8

French Cherry Tart

2 eggs
1/2 cup caster sugar
4 tablespoons ground
  almonds
2 tablespoons sour cream
1 × 810 g can pitted black
  cherries, drained
1 x 22 cm pastry crust
1/2 teaspoon nutmeg
whipped cream

TIME: 21 MINUTES

Beat together eggs, caster sugar, 2 tablespoons ground almonds and sour cream till fluffy.

Arrange cherries in a layer on base of pie crust. Pour over egg mixture. Sprinkle remaining almonds and nutmeg over pie. Cook on MEDIUM 15–20 minutes. Stand 5 minutes. Serve with whipped cream.

Serves 6–8

1. Beat together eggs, caster sugar, almonds and sour cream

2. Arrange cherries in pie crust

French Cherry Tart   3. Pour egg mixture over cherries

Rhubarb Pie

750 g rhubarb, cut into
    2.5 cm lengths
1/2–3/4 cup sugar
2 tablespoons custard
    powder
pinch salt
1 teaspoon mixed spice
1/2 cup raisins

Pastry

1 1/2 cups flour
1 teaspoon baking powder
1/2 teaspoon salt
125 g butter, cut in small
    cubes
2 teaspoons sugar
3–4 tablespoons cold water
1 tablespoon sugar

TIME: 17–20 MINUTES

Combine rhubarb, sugar, custard powder, salt, mixed spice and raisins in a bowl.

Sift flour, baking powder and salt and place in food processor. Add butter and 2 teaspoons sugar and blend to a crumb texture, adding water gradually until dough forms a ball. Chill pastry 15–20 minutes.

Roll out two-thirds of pastry, line 23 cm pie plate and place rhubarb mixture onto pastry, piling centre high. Roll out remaining pastry and brush edge of pastry in pie plate with cold water. Place remaining pastry over rhubarb and seal edges. Cut air vents in top, brush with water and sprinkle with 1 tablespoon sugar.

Cook on HIGH 8 minutes, then convection at 200°C (400°F) 7–10 minutes until pastry is well browned. Serve with cream or custard sauce.

Serves 6–8

Hazelnut Pie

Filling

3 eggs
1/2 cup brown sugar
1 cup corn syrup
40 g butter
1 tablespoon flour
1 teaspoon vanilla essence
1/4 teaspoon salt
1 cup roughly chopped
    roasted hazelnuts

Pastry

1 cup flour
1/2 teaspoon salt
80 g cooking margarine
40 g butter
3 tablespoons cold water

TIME: 18 MINUTES

To make pastry, combine flour and salt in a medium-sized bowl. Cut in margarine and butter to resemble coarse crumbs. Blend in water and knead lightly. Let rest in refrigerator 15 minutes. Roll out, line a 22 cm pie plate and chill a further 10 minutes.

Beat 1 egg yolk lightly and brush evenly over prepared pastry case to seal. Cook on HIGH 45 seconds until yolk has set.

Combine in mixing bowl remaining eggs — separated white and leftover beaten yolk. Add remaining ingredients except hazelnuts. Blend well. Stir in hazelnuts and cook on HIGH 4 minutes, stirring after 2 minutes.

Pour into pastry case. Reduce power to MEDIUM and cook 10–13 minutes until filling has almost set. Let stand 6 minutes before serving. The standing time completes the cooking.

Serve hot or cold with whipped cream.

Serves 6–8

Note: This pie can also be made with walnuts or pecans. If corn syrup is unavailable, substitute with golden or maple syrup.

Hazelnut Pie

2. *Combine filling ingredients*

3. *Pour cooked filling into pastry crust*

MILK AND EGG DESSERTS

Who would ever have thought that such a startling variety of desserts can be conjured up from these two simple primary products? With just a few additional ingredients, we show you how to make an inviting selection of dishes that will delight family and friends alike.

Tropical Creme Caramel

Tropical Creme Caramel

A variation of a traditional dessert — a creme caramel served with avocado and tropical fruits. This recipe can be made a day ahead.

Caramel

¾ cup raw sugar
1 cup water

Custard

4 eggs
2 egg yolks
1 teaspoon vanilla essence or
  vanilla bean
300 mL cream, whipped
¼ cup raw sugar
1½ cups mashed avocado
2 cups milk

Topping

¼ avocado, finely sliced
½ mango, finely diced
½ kiwifruit, finely sliced
½ large banana, finely sliced
1 teaspoon finely sliced
  pawpaw

Stir sugar and water over low heat until sugar dissolves. Bring to boil, without stirring, and cook until a rich golden brown. Don't stir.

Pour caramel evenly into individual souffle dishes and, working quickly, revolve dishes in order to coat sides and base.

Use an oven glove as dishes become quite hot when coating with caramel.

Place eggs, egg yolks, vanilla and sugar in a bowl and beat together lightly. Beat in mashed avocado until smooth and creamy.

Heat milk and bring to just below boiling point. (If using vanilla bean, heat bean with milk.) Cool 10 minutes and add vanilla essence.

Pour milk over egg and avocado mixture, stirring constantly. Strain if any large lumps occur.

Place caramel-lined dishes in a baking tray. Add water to tray so that it is half-way up sides of dishes. Pour in custard and bake in 160°C (310°F) oven for about 30 to 35 minutes or until custard is set.

Cover each dish with foil and refrigerate several hours before serving.

Combine fruit together. To serve, ease custard away from sides of dish with a knife. Turn out onto individual small plates or saucers. Decorate with whipped cream piped around edge of custard. Fill centre with colourful array of chopped fruits.

Serves 6

Fruit Brulee

4 cups prepared fruit
1 cup cream
4 tablespoons brown sugar
¼ teaspoon cinnamon

Use any fruit in season for this dessert, such as grapes, peeled and seeded; cherries, seeded; apricots, quartered; strawberries, hulled; kiwifruit, peeled and sliced.

Place fruit into 4 individual serving dishes and pour ¼ cup cream into each. Leave in refrigerator overnight. Just before serving sprinkle 1 tablespoon brown sugar and a little cinnamon over each and place under griller until sugar melts and browns.

Serves 4

1. Turn dishes to coat sides and base with caramel

2. Pour milk over egg and avocado mixture

3. Pour custard into dishes prior to baking

Creme Brulee

The cream for this is better prepared the day before it is needed.

500 mL cream
1 vanilla pod, split
4 egg yolks
4½ tablespoons caster sugar

Set the oven at 170°C (325°F). Put the cream and vanilla pod in the top of a double boiler, cover and bring to scalding point. Meanwhile work yolks and 1 tablespoon of the sugar with a wooden spoon until light in colour. Remove vanilla pod and pour the cream on to the egg yolks and sugar and mix well; return mixture to the pan and thicken very carefully over the heat, stirring continuously. The mixture should coat the back of a wooden spoon, but must not boil.

Strain the mixture into a shallow ovenproof dish and place in a very moderate oven for 5–8 minutes, until a skin forms on the top. Allow cream to stand in a cool place for several hours or preferably overnight.

To finish the cream, preheat grill, dust top of cream evenly with remaining sugar and slip it under grill at least 10 cm away from the heat. At this distance the sugar has a chance to melt before it begins to brown and an even coating of caramel over the cream is ensured. Remove the cream from under the grill and let it stand in the refrigerator for 2–3 hours before serving. A bowl of sugared fruit — raspberries, strawberries or tropical fruits can be served separately and makes a good contrast to the rich cream.

Citrus Souffle

4 large oranges, limes or
 lemons
½ cup sugar
2 eggs (separated)
1 tablespoon Grand Marnier
 (optional)

Cut tops off fruit and remove all flesh. Ensure they are totally dry. Finely grate rind from removed tops and reserve. Discard pips and blend in processor.

Strain into small pan and boil with the liqueur for 3–4 minutes reducing liquid to ⅓ cup. Add sugar and dissolve over heat, then cool. Place liquid in processor, add rind, egg yolks, and blend.

Whip egg whites separately until stiff. Blend a little egg white into mixture to aerate, then pour in remainder. Fill into shells and place in centre of oven but not on trays. Cook 15 minutes at 180°C (350°F) and serve immediately.

Serves 4

Date Souffle with Orange Sauce

½ cup fresh dates, stoned
½ flour
60 g butter, softened
1 cup milk
2 tablespoons finely grated
 orange rind
3 eggs, separated
3 tablespoons sugar

Orange Sauce

¼ cup sugar
1 tablespoon cornflour
1 cup orange juice
2 tablespoons finely grated
 orange rind
⅓ cup cream

Puree dates in blender or food processor. Mix with flour and butter. Heat milk until nearly boiling and gradually stir into date mixture. Cook over hot water about 5 minutes, stirring constantly. Add orange rind. Beat egg yolks until thick and beat in sugar gradually. Stir in hot mixture slowly. Cool. Fold in stiffly beaten egg whites, pour into greased souffle dish, place in pan of hot water and bake at 160°C (325°F) for 1 hour until set.

Meanwhile, mix sugar and cornflour in saucepan. Add orange juice and rind and cook over medium heat, stirring constantly. Cover and cook over boiling water 10 minutes longer. Just before serving, stir in cream. Serve the sauce with the souffle.

Serves 6

Ginger Souffle

60 g butter
3 tablespoons flour
1½ cups milk
2 tablespoons sugar
3 eggs

1 teaspoon vanilla essence
2 teaspoons grated ginger in
 syrup
icing sugar

Melt butter in saucepan, stir in flour and cook 1 minute. Add milk gradually to form a smooth sauce. Stir until sauce thickens and boils. Stir in sugar until dissolved. Cool sauce slightly.

Separate eggs and beat yolks into sauce with vanilla essence and grated ginger. Beat egg whites until stiff and fold in sauce. Spoon mixture into souffle dish and bake at 190°C (375°F) for 40 minutes. Sprinkle with sieved icing sugar and serve immediately.

Serves 4–6

SUCCESSFUL SOUFFLES
☐ Have the oven heated to the right temperature well before the souffle goes into the oven.
☐ Make sure the eggs are at room temperature before whisking.
☐ Remove all trace of egg yolk from the whites before mixing.
☐ Use a large copper or metal bowl and balloon whisk to give the egg whites greater volume and density.
☐ Fold the stiff egg whites into the mixture very gently in long circular strokes, turning the bowl in a circular motion at the same time.
☐ Once the egg whites have been whisked, do not leave them to sit, fold them into the sauce and put into the oven immediately.

Lemon-Avocado Souffle

A rich, beautiful and tasty end to a meal.

1 cup raw sugar
2 lemons
4 egg yolks
6 egg whites
3 avocados
2 tablespoons gelatine or
    agar-agar
300 mL whipped cream
avocado slices and a lemon
    twist to garnish

Beat egg yolks and sugar together. Grate rinds of lemons and squeeze the juice. Add rind and 6 tablespoons of lemon juice to egg yolks, beating constantly.

Soften gelatine in 6 tablespoons water and heat until it is liquid. Do the same if using agar-agar. Cool slightly.

Whip cream and beat into mashed avocados. Then stir into lemon and egg mixture.

Stir in gelatine and continue until it begins to thicken.

Beat egg whites until soft peaks form. Fold into lemon and avocado mixture.

Spoon carefully into a souffle dish or tall parfait glasses and chill until set.

Serves 10

Note: This souffle can be served with extra whipped cream and garnished with avocado slices, a lemon twist and a sprig of mint.

Frozen Irish Coffee Mousse

3 egg yolks
1/2 cup sugar
1 tablespoon instant coffee,
    dissolved in 1 tablespoon
    hot water
1 cup cream, whipped
1 tablespoon Irish whiskey
1 1/2 cups fromage blanc (see
    recipe)
1 tablespoon honey
1/2 teaspoon vanilla essence
2 egg whites

Whisk egg yolks, sugar and dissolved coffee over bain-marie until light and creamy with sugar dissolved. Remove and continue to whisk until cool. Fold in whiskey and cream.

Blend fromage blanc, honey and vanilla essence. Add to mousse. Whip egg whites until firm but not stiff and fold into mixture. Pour into metal tray. Leave until almost set, turn into bowl and whisk to increase volume. Return to tray and allow to freeze 1 hour before serving.

Prepare topping: pour 1 cup black coffee into metal tray and freeze. As it freezes, fork around to form tiny crystals. When frozen sprinkle these on top of mousse to serve.

Serves 6-8

Sun Glory Pawpaw Pudding

300 mL milk
1/3 cup semolina
2 tablespoons gelatine
2 tablespoons honey
juice and grated rind 1
    lemon
juice and grated rind 1
    orange
1 cup pawpaw pulp
150 mL cream

Garnish

1 pawpaw
2 limes or lemons, thinly
    sliced

Boil milk, stir in semolina and cook 5 minutes. Blend gelatine and honey, stir in hot semolina mixture until dissolved. Flavour with lemon and orange rind and juice, stir in pawpaw and cool.

Whip cream and fold into mixture. Pour into greased 23 cm ring mould. Leave to set in refrigerator for 3-4 hours.

Turn pudding onto serving dish. Scoop out flesh from pawpaw with melon ball cutter and pile into centre. Arrange lime slices around outside, overlapping each other.

Serves 6

Hint: If pawpaw not available, substitute any melon. When grating rind from lemon or orange, do so gently as only the colour is wanted. The white pith is bitter.

Baked Apple and Sago Pudding

600 mL milk
1/4 cup sago
3 eggs
2 tablespoons honey
1/8 teaspoon ground nutmeg
1/8 teaspoon ground cloves
2 apples, peeled, cored and
    sliced
2 tablespoons butter

Bring milk and sago to boil and cook 8 minutes. Leave to cool. Beat in eggs, honey and spices. Gently cook apples in butter until soft. Arrange in souffle dish and fill dish with sago mixture.

Place dish in baking tray half filled with hot water and bake at 180°C (350°F) for 45 minutes. Serve cold.

Serves 4

Sun Glory Pawpaw Pudding (left) and Baked Apple and Sago Pudding

Almond Float

2½ cups milk
¼ cup sugar
almond essence to taste
1½ tablespoons gelatine
½ cup water
selection of fresh fruit,
    prepared
1 × 425 g can lychees

Scald the milk, remove from heat and add the sugar. Cool slightly then add the almond essence. Cool. Meanwhile, sprinkle the gelatine over the water and leave until the water has absorbed. Dissolve the gelatine over hot water and cool. Stir into the milk mixture. Cool, then chill until set.

When ready to serve, cut the almond gelatine into diamond shapes. Place the fruit in a serving bowl. Place the diamonds on top and serve.

Serves 4

Quick Lemon Syllabub

A syllabub is whipped flavoured cream

4 tablespoons dry white wine
finely-grated rind and juice
    of 1 large lemon
2½ tablespoons caster sugar
300 mL cream

Put the wine, lemon rind and juice and sugar into a bowl. Stir to blend the ingredients, then pour in the cream and whisk until the mixture is light and thick. Pour the syllabub into individual goblets and chill well. Serve with sponge fingers, if wished.

Serves 2

Drambuie Orange Syllabub

3 oranges
3 tablespoons chopped dried
    apricots
4 tablespoons Drambuie
½ cup caster sugar
1¾ cups cream
2½ tablespoons grated
    orange rind

Thinly peel the rind of 1½ oranges and place with the apricots in a small bowl. Cover with the squeezed juice of the 3 oranges and the Drambuie. Leave to macerate overnight.

Next day, remove the orange rind and apricots and stir in the sugar. Slowly stir in the cream and then whisk until the syllabub stands in soft peaks. Divide the reserved chopped apricots between 4 tall glasses and spoon in the syllabub. Sprinkle a little grated orange rind over the top of each one and serve with shortcake biscuits.

Serves 4

Note: You can vary the flavour of this delicious dessert by experimenting with different spirits and liqueurs. Try Scotch whisky or an orange liqueur such as Cointreau.

Hazelnut Ice Cream

4 egg yolks
¾ cup sugar
1 cup ground hazelnuts
2 cups milk

Bring the milk to the boil, stir in the hazelnuts and let it infuse until the milk gets cold. Strain through muslin or a very fine sieve.

Beat the egg yolks with the sugar until creamy and forming a ribbon. Add the milk and put in the top of a double boiler on low heat. Continue to beat until it reaches boiling point. Let it get cold.

If you have an ice cream maker, pour the mixture into it and churn until frozen. Otherwise, pour the mixture into ice cube trays and place in the freezer. Stir it through after the first hour, to break up any ice particles that might have formed, and finish the freezing process. Serve with crostoli (see recipe).

Serves 4

Zabaglione Ice Cream

4 egg yolks
¾ cup sugar
2 cups milk
⅓ cup Marsala

In a bowl, beat the yolks with the sugar until creamy and forming a ribbon. Place the bowl in a double boiler, add the milk and continue beating until very hot. Let the mixture cool.

If you have an ice cream maker, pour the mixture into it and churn until frozen. Otherwise, pour the mixture into ice cube trays and place in the freezer. Stir it through after the first hour, to break up any ice particles that might have formed, and finish the freezing process. Serve with crostoli (see recipe).

Serves 4

Peach and Buttermilk Ice Cream

1 × 450 g can sliced peaches
    in syrup
3 tablespoons lemon juice
good pinch salt
1½ cups buttermilk
6 pieces bottled stem ginger,
    chopped

Drain the peaches and liquidise the fruit to a puree. Mix the peach puree with the lemon juice, salt and buttermilk, pour into a freezer tray and freeze. When the mixture is half frozen, mix in the preserved ginger and refreeze.

Serves 4–6

Green-with-Envy Cheesecake

Green-with-Envy Cheesecake

Cheesecake is loved by all, and with this avocado filling it will be even more popular.

2 cups fine biscuit crumbs
½ cup melted butter
3 tablespoons raw sugar
500 g cream cheese
3 avocados
1 cup cream
3 eggs
1 cup honey or raw sugar
½ teaspoon cinnamon
1 teaspoon vanilla essence
¼ cup brandy
whipped cream and kiwi-
*   fruit slices to garnish*

Mix biscuit crumbs with the melted butter and sugar, working it together with your fingers. Press into well-greased spring-form tin and, using a masher, make a flat, smooth crust.

Beat cream cheese with avocados, cream, eggs, honey or sugar until smooth. This can be done in a blender, electric mixer or food processor. Add cinnamon, vanilla and brandy.

Pour mixture into prepared spring-form pan and bake at 160°C (310°F) for about 1 hour.

Cool, refrigerate and garnish with whipped cream and kiwifruit before serving.

Serves 12

Apricot Cheesecake

Cheesecakes freeze particularly well. Freeze it until you need it — and decorate just before serving with fruit, cream or glaze.

1 × 425 g can apricots in
*   syrup*
1 packet orange jelly
450 g cottage cheese
5 teaspoons caster sugar
150 mL cream, whipped
100 g ginger biscuits,
*   crushed*
5 teaspoons sugar
50 g butter, melted

Garnish

2 tablespoons apricot jam
1 × 425 g can apricots in
*   syrup*
1 tablespoon flaked almonds

Make up the syrup from the canned apricots with water to 300 mL. Bring to the boil, add the jelly and stir to dissolve. Cool. Sieve the apricots and cheese and stir in the cooled jelly and sugar. Fold in the cream.

Line the base of a 20 cm cake tin with non-stick paper. Pour in the mixture and chill to set. Freeze until needed. Combine the biscuits, sugar and butter, sprinkle over the set mixture and press down with a spoon.

Melt the jam with 1 tablespoon of the apricot syrup, sieve and cool. Turn out the cheesecake and decorate with the apricots. Brush with the jam glaze and sprinkle with almonds.

Frozen Yoghurt Ambrosia

The topping can be made well in advance and stored in an airtight jar.

2/3 cup cream
1/2 cup caster sugar
1 teaspoon vanilla essence
1 cup natural yoghurt

Topping

3 tablespoons sunflower
  seeds
3 tablespoons chopped
  hazelnuts
3 tablespoons roughly
  chopped walnuts
1 tablespoon desiccated
  coconut
1/2 cup dried apple rings,
  roughly chopped
1/2 cup dried peaches or
  apricots, roughly chopped

Whip the cream until it is just thick, and fold in the sugar, vanilla and yoghurt. Transfer the mixture to a polythene freezer container and place it in the freezer for 1–2 hours, until the mixture is icy around the edges. Whisk until smooth, then return to the freezer until firm.

To make topping, lightly toast the sunflower seeds and mix with the remaining topping ingredients. Allow the ice cream to soften in the refrigerator for 30 minutes before serving. Scoop the ice cream into 4–6 dessert glasses and sprinkle with the topping. Serve immediately.

Serves 4–6

Coconut Cream Custard

1 cup brown sugar
1/4 cup water
2 cups coconut milk
4 eggs
1/2 teaspoon ground
  cardamom
1/4 teaspoon nutmeg

Place sugar and water in saucepan and heat until sugar dissolves. Cool. Combine syrup with remaining ingredients and strain.

Pour into individual cups and place in baking dish. Add a little cold water to baking dish and bake at 180°C (350°F) for 1 hour or until custard is set. Cool, run knife round edge and turn out to serve.

Serves 4–6

Note: To make coconut milk place 2 cups desiccated coconut in a blender with 2 1/4 cups hot water. Blend until smooth, strain through fine sieve and use liquid.

Parsee Custard

This sweet is eaten at Parsee weddings.

3 1/2 cups milk
3 tablespoons caster sugar
5 eggs
1 tablespoon ground
  almonds
1 tablespoon rose water
pinch nutmeg and
  cardamom powder

Boil the milk and sugar together on a low heat till quantity is reduced to half.

Allow to cool a little and gradually add 3 whole eggs plus 2 egg yolks, well beaten together. Add the almonds and rose water.

Pour the custard into a dish and sprinkle with nutmeg and cardamom powders.

Pre-heat the oven to 200°C (400°F). Place dish in a pan of hot water, and bake for 45 minutes to 1 hour till the custard is set.

Serves 6–8

Zabaglione

4 egg yolks
1/2 cup sugar
grated peel of half a lemon
2/3 cup dry Marsala

Put the egg yolks and sugar in a bowl and beat until the mixture forms a ribbon. Add the lemon peel and Marsala and place the bowl over heat in a double boiler. Keep beating with a whisk or egg beater until you have obtained a rich, frothy consistency, and the volume of the eggs has doubled.

Pour into wine glasses and serve hot. Accompany with homemade biscuits, such as Almond Tuile Biscuits *(see recipe)*.

Serves 4

Almond Tuile Biscuits

75 g butter
1/3 cup caster sugar
1/3 cup flour
pinch salt
1/3 cup almonds, finely
  chopped

Preheat the oven to 200°C (400°F). Cream the butter and sugar until light and fluffy. Sieve flour and salt and stir into creamed mixture with the almonds.

Place a teaspoonful of the mixture on a well-greased baking sheet and flatten with a wet fork. Repeat with 3 more teaspoonfuls and bake for 6–8 minutes until lightly coloured. Allow to stand for a second or two, then remove with a sharp knife and curl on a rolling pin until set.

Repeat the process until all of the mixture has been used.

Makes 12 biscuits

Chocolate Souffle

Chocolate Flake Cheesecake

1½ cups semi-sweet biscuit
    crumbs
2 tablespoons sugar
½ teaspoon cinnamon
½ teaspoon nutmeg
125 g butter, melted
4 cups cream-style cottage
    cheese
1 cup sour cream
6 eggs, beaten
1½ cups sugar
½ cup flour
pinch salt
3 chocolate flake bars,
    crumbled
1 teaspoon rum essence   TIME: 23 MINUTES

Combine semi-sweet biscuit crumbs, sugar, cinnamon, nutmeg and butter. Press mixture into base and sides of 25 cm cake dish. Cook on HIGH 3 minutes. Chill till set.

Combine cottage cheese, sour cream, eggs and sugar. Beat thoroughly. Fold in sifted flour and salt. Fold in 2 flake bars and rum essence. Pour mixture into biscuit crust. Cook on MEDIUM 15–20 minutes. Stand 10 minutes. Decorate with extra flake bar. Serve cold.

Serves 8–10

Chocolate Souffle

6 teaspoons gelatine
¾ cup sugar
3 eggs, separated
1 cup milk
60 g cooking chocolate (chop
    or grate chocolate, and
    cook ¾–1 minute to melt)
1 cup whipped cream   TIME: 7½ MINUTES

In a large bowl combine gelatine with ½ cup sugar. Stir in egg yolks and beat in the milk. Heat on DEFROST 6½–7½ minutes or until gelatine dissolves, stirring occasionally. Add chocolate and chill, stirring occasionally until mixture mounds slightly.

Beat egg whites until soft peaks form, gradually add remaining sugar and beat until stiff. Fold in the chocolate mixture with whipped cream. Pour into a souffle dish with a collar. Chill. To serve, garnish with extra whipped cream and almond slivers.

Serves 6

Pistachio Orange Souffle

10 eggs, separated
2 cups sugar
½ cup orange juice
½ cup lime juice
grated rind 2 oranges
2 tablespoons gelatine
¼ cup water
pinch salt
2 cups cream
½ cup pistachio nuts,
    crushed

Garnish
orange slices
extra crushed pistachio nuts   TIME: 5½ MINUTES

Place egg yolks in mixing bowl and beat with electric mixer until fluffy. Add sugar and continue to beat till creamy. Cook on HIGH 4 minutes, stirring occasionally. Add orange, lime juice and rind and blend thoroughly. Set aside.

Place gelatine and water into small bowl and cook on HIGH 1½ minutes. Stir and set aside to cool. Whisk egg whites till stiff then add pinch salt. Whip cream.

Fold together gelatine, egg yolk mixture, egg whites and cream. Divide mixture between 6 individual 200 mL souffle dishes and chill for 2 hours.

Decorate with orange slices and crushed pistachio nuts.

Serves 6

Savarin

60 g butter, softened
½ cup caster sugar
3 eggs
1 cup self-raising flour
2 tablespoons milk or cream

Syrup
1 cup sugar
1 cup water
⅓ cup Grand Marnier   TIME: 6 MINUTES

Beat softened butter and sugar to a cream. Add eggs, one at a time. Add flour, all at once. Fold in milk or cream. Grease and line base of micro-ring dish. Grease again. Pour in mixture and cook 5–6 minutes on HIGH. Turn out on a cooking rack.

Boil sugar and water to form a syrup. Add Grand Marnier. Spoon warm syrup over cake until all of it has been absorbed. Place onto a serving platter. Fill centre with fresh fruit salad. Decorate with whipped cream and extra fruit.

Serves 8

Strawberry Kahlua Mousse

Strawberry Kahlua Mousse

Mousse

½ cup sugar
3 teaspoons gelatine
2 tablespoons water
1 cup milk
4 egg yolks
1 tablespoon Kahlua
250 g strawberries, hulled
    and chopped
300 mL thickened cream

Strawberry Kahlua Sauce

¼ cup Kahlua
1 tablespoon sugar
12 strawberries, hulled and
    chopped finely

TIME: 13 MINUTES

Combine sugar, gelatine and water in a small bowl. Cook on HIGH 30–60 seconds. Allow to cool slightly.

Combine milk, egg yolks, Kahlua and strawberries in mixing bowl. Cook on MEDIUM 5–7 minutes, stirring occasionally until thickened. Set aside.

Whip cream until stiff. Fold gelatine, strawberry mixture and cream together. Pour into 1 litre mould and chill. When firm, unmould onto serving plate.

Combine sauce ingredients in a bowl and cook on high 5 minutes. Serve with the mousse.

Serves 4–6

1. *Combine sugar, gelatine and water and cook on high*

2. *Mix milk, yolks, Kahlua and strawberries*

3. *Fold together gelatine, strawberry mixture and whipped cream*

Egg Custard

3 tablespoons sugar
1 tablespoon flour
½ cup milk
½ cup cream
6 egg yolks
1 teaspoon Grand Marnier
1–2 teaspoons caster sugar

TIME: 3 MINUTES

Combine sugar and flour in a bowl and beat in milk and cream. Cook on HIGH 2 minutes, stirring every 30 seconds. Beat egg yolks, add to milk and cream sauce.

Cook on HIGH 30–45 seconds, stirring after each 15 seconds. Beat in Grand Marnier. Sprinkle lightly with a little caster sugar to prevent a skin forming on the sauce.

Makes about 2 cups

1. *Spread meringue evenly into tray*

Pavlova Roll

2 teaspoons melted butter
2 teaspoons cornflour
6 egg whites
1½ cups caster sugar
¾ teaspoon vanilla essence
1 teaspoon white vinegar
½ cup toasted almond
   slivers
1 tablespoon cinnamon
   sugar
2 cups fresh strawberries
300 mL cream, whipped

TIME: 3 MINUTES

Place butter in small bowl and cook on high 15 seconds to melt. Lightly grease tray and line base with greaseproof paper. Regrease and dust lightly with cornflour and shake off excess.

Beat egg whites until firm peaks form. Add sugar, one tablespoon at a time, beating until dissolved. Blend in vanilla and vinegar.

Spread meringue evenly into prepared 30 x 30 cm tray and sprinkle with toasted almonds. Cook on HIGH 3 minutes and allow to cool.

Sprinkle a large sheet of greaseproof paper with cinnamon sugar and turn pavlova onto it. Slice 1½ cups of strawberries and fold into whipped cream. Spread cream over two-thirds of the pavlova.

Roll up as for a Swiss roll. Pipe rosettes of cream on top and garnish with remaining strawberries, cut into fans. Chill before serving.

Serves 6–8

STRAWBERRY FANS
Wash and hull strawberries and with a sharp, thin-bladed knife make 5–6 cuts into each strawberry. These cuts should extend only ⅔ into the strawberry from the top. Carefully separate slices till the strawberry takes on a fan-shape.

Pavlova Roll

2. *Sprinkle with roasted almonds*

3. *Roll up pavlova with greaseproof paper*

DINNER PARTY DESSERTS

This section caters for all those occasions when a spectacular dessert is called for — from exotic fruit ice-creams to light, cream filled profiteroles which will be the highlight of any event.

Profiteroles

Mother's Tried and True Pavlova

The famous Australian dessert was invented in 1935 by Bert Sachse, a chef at Perth's Esplanade Hotel. A member of staff named it after the famous Russian ballerina.

4 egg whites, at room
   temperature
1 cup caster sugar
½ teaspoon vanilla
¾ teaspoon white vinegar

Filling

300 mL thickened cream,
   whipped
1 punnet strawberries or 5
   passionfruit

Preheat the oven to maximum temperature. Use the small bowl of an electric mixer and ensure that it is clean and dry.

Place egg whites in the bowl and beat until soft peaks form. Add ⅓ cup of sugar and beat until dissolved. This can be tested by rubbing a small amount of mixture between your fingers; it should feel velvety and not gritty.

Gradually add remaining sugar, beating well after each addition.

When the sugar has dissolved add the vanilla and vinegar and beat slowly for one minute or until combined. Line a baking tray with lightly greased foil. Dust the foil lightly with cornflour. Mark an 18 cm circle on the foil. Spoon the meringue into the centre of the circle and spread to the edges using soft strokes with a spatula. Don't flatten the meringue, leave a 5 cm high edge and a slight depression in the centre.

Reduce the oven temperature to lowest possible and bake Pavlova for 1½ hours or until firm to touch. Turn the oven off, leave the door ajar and allow Pavlova to cool for several hours. This slow cooling prevents cracking.

Just before serving, spoon the whipped cream into the centre of the Pavlova and decorate with the rinsed and drained strawberries or passionfruit pulp or both!

Serves 12

Chocolate Mousse

A mousse is more elaborate than a syllabub. This rich mousse is set with egg whites rather than gelatine and is served with biscuits called Cigarettes Russes.

175 g plain block chocolate
2–3 tablespoons black coffee
   or water
15 g butter
2 teaspoons rum, or 2–3
   drops vanilla essence
3 eggs
1 × 300 mL carton cream
   (optional)

Break the chocolate into small pieces, put into a pan with the coffee and stir continually over a gentle heat to a thick cream. The chocolate should be hot but the sides of the pan never so hot that you cannot touch them. Take off the heat, stir in the butter and flavouring.

Crack each of the eggs, putting the whites into a basin and dropping the yolks, one at a time, into the chocolate; stir well after each addition. It is important that the chocolate is hot when the yolks go in so that they cook slightly.

Whisk the whites to firm peaks, then stir briskly into the chocolate. When thoroughly mixed fill 4–6 small pots and leave overnight in the larder or refrigerator. For easy pouring turn the mixture first into a jug, scraping the pan out well. Mousses can be served plain with biscuits, or whipped cream can be spooned, or piped (with a rose nozzle and forcing bag, preferably of nylon), on top of each mousse. If cream is used, you could put a biscuit in the centre of each one just before serving.

Serves 4–6

Cigarettes Russes

2 egg whites
½ cup caster sugar
50 g butter
⅓ cup flour, sifted
2–3 drops of vanilla essence

Break the egg whites into a basin, add the sugar and beat with a fork until smooth. Melt the butter and add with the sifted flour to the mixture. Flavour with 2–3 drops of vanilla essence.

Spread the mixture in oblongs on the greased and floured baking sheet and bake for 5–6 minutes in an oven at 200°C (400°F). (It is a good idea to test mixture by baking one only at first. If difficult to handle, add a pinch of flour, or if too firm and hard, you can add 2 teaspoons of melted butter.)

Take the oblongs out of the oven and allow to stand for 1–2 seconds, then remove them with a sharp knife, placing them upside down on the table. Roll each one tightly round a wooden spoon handle, skewer or pencil, holding it firmly with your hand. Remove at once from the spoon, and allow to cool. Store in an airtight tin.

Makes about 00

Mother's Tried and True Pavlova

Profiteroles

Profiteroles are a mouth-watering combination of choux pastry, with pastry cream and chocolate sauce. The following three recipes can be used in a variety of ways to create spectacular dinner party desserts.

Choux Pastry

50 g butter
1½ teaspoons sugar
¼ cup water
¼ cup milk
½ cup flour
pinch of salt
2 eggs, lightly beaten
icing sugar for dusting

Set oven at 220°C (425°F). Grease and flour baking trays. Place butter, sugar, water and milk into small saucepan. Dissolve butter and bring to boil. Immediately add sifted flour and salt together. Stir quickly with wooden spoon until mixture leaves sides and rolls into a ball. Stir over heat 1 minute. Allow to cool, then beat vigorously for few seconds. Slowly add eggs one at a time and beating constantly until mixture is glossy and drops from a spoon.

Using 2 teaspoons or piping bag, place small amounts on prepared trays. Sieve a little icing sugar over. Bake in oven 15 minutes, then reduce heat to 200°C (400°F) and bake for further 10 minutes or until firm.

Makes 40 small puffs or one large ring

Pastry Cream

Pastry Cream is used as a filling for profiteroles, any choux pastry dessert, or for fruit flans. Layer into puff pastry with whipped cream, jam or fruit; use as a filling for pancakes or serve hot as a creamy custard.

4 egg yolks
½ cup caster sugar
⅔ cup flour
vanilla essence
2 cups milk

Cream together yolks, sugar and flour in basin with vanilla. Parboil milk, whisk in to the yolk mixture and return to saucepan. Bring to boil, whisking continuously until the sauce boils and thickens. Cook 2 minutes and stir to cool.

Cover with plastic to prevent skin from forming and store in refrigerator.

When cooled, pastry cream may be enriched with extra cream, lightly whipped, or made lighter with the addition of a stiffly beaten egg white.

Profiteroles

Chocolate Sauce

175 g dark chocolate
½ cup sugar
2 cups water

Cut the chocolate into small pieces and melt it in a bowl over a pan of hot water. Heat the sugar and water in a saucepan, stirring continuously until the sugar dissolves. Boil the syrup gently for 5 minutes.

Carefully stir the sugar syrup into the chocolate. Return the mixture to the saucepan and, stirring continuously bring it to a simmer. Let it simmer for 7–10 minutes or until the sauce thickly coats the back of a wooden spoon.

Makes 2 cups

CHOUX SHUFFLE

Serving suggestions: These three basic recipes can be used to make a variety of delightful desserts.
- ☐ Shape the choux into balls, fill with cream and coat in chocolate sauce.
- ☐ Pipe the choux into a ring, fill it with pastry cream or fresh cream, then decorate the centre with seasonal fruit garnished with icing sugar.
- ☐ Pipe the choux into strips, fill them with fresh cream and ice with chocolate, coffee or orange liqueur icing to make eclairs.
- ☐ To make Croquembouche, the traditional French wedding cake, make choux balls, fill with pastry cream and pile into a conical shape on a round base of sweet pastry, securing the balls with hot caramel sugar, then decorate with spun sugar.

Marinated Rock Melon

1 rock melon
4 tablespoons Marsala or port
1 tablespoon sugar
1 punnet raspberries
   (optional)

With a melon baller, scoop out melon flesh and transfer to a glass bowl. Add raspberries if using, sprinkle with sugar and Marsala or port and chill before serving.

Serves 4

Nectarines with Pecan Topping

4 nectarines, halved and
   stoned
1 tablespoon rum
½ cup chopped pecans
2 tablespoons brown sugar
2 teaspoons butter, softened
2 teaspoons flour

Arrange nectarines cut side up in baking dish and sprinkle with rum. Mix pecans, brown sugar, butter and flour to a paste and divide between nectarines. Press gently to fill hollows; level top. Grill for 4 minutes until topping is brown and bubbly.

Serves 4

Orange and Rhubarb Compote

1 bunch rhubarb
2 oranges
½ cup brown sugar
¼ cup water

Wash rhubarb and trim stalks. Cut into 3 cm lengths. Peel oranges, making sure all pith is removed. Cut into thin rounds and remove all pips. Layer fruit into baking dish and sprinkle with sugar. Add water, cover and bake at 180°C (350°F) until rhubarb is tender. Serve hot or cold.

Serves 4

Pineapple Sorbet

Pineapple Sorbet

1 medium pineapple
2 limes
1 ½ cups water
¾ cup caster sugar
mint sprigs for garnish

Cut pineapple in half lengthwise; leave leaves intact. Using grapefruit knife, remove the flesh, leaving shells whole for serving. Place pineapple shells in refrigerator until needed. Peel limes, removing white pith, cut in quarters. Puree lime and pineapple fruits in blender or food processor.

Simmer water and sugar for 8–10 minutes until sugar has dissolved and thin syrup forms. Allow to cool then add to pineapple mixture. Pour into freezer trays and freeze until set. Puree again in blender. Pour back into freezer trays, cover with foil and allow to refreeze.

When ready to serve, dip bottom of trays in hot water, tip out sorbet and cut into large dice. Pile sorbet into pineapple shells and serve. Garnish with mint sprigs.

Serves 6

1. Remove flesh using grapefruit knife

2. Peel limes and cut into quarters

3. Pour syrup into pureed fruit

Pears in White Wine

12 small cooking pears,
  peeled (leave stems on)
½ cup honey
1 cup white wine
1 cup water
1 lemon
1 stick cinnamon
4 whole cloves

Arrange pears in shallow ovenproof dish. Boil honey, wine and water together for 3 minutes and pour over pears. Slice the lemon and add to dish with spices. Cover and bake at 180°C (350°F) for 1 hour, turning pears occasionally. Leave to cool.

Arrange pears in serving dish, strain juice and pour around pears.

Serves 6

Stewed Prickly Pears

1 cup sugar
2½ cups water
few drops cochineal
16 prickly pears, peeled
juice 1 lemon
icing sugar

Boil sugar and water until thin syrup forms. Add cochineal and stir well. Add pears and simmer for 3 minutes. Stir in lemon juice and chill thoroughly. Sprinkle with icing sugar. Serve with chilled custard.

Serves 4

Note: Gloves are essential for peeling prickly pears. Do not discard the seeds as they are edible.

Peaches in Spumante

4 perfectly matured
  freestone peaches
a little icing sugar
1 × 750 mL bottle good
  quality dry Italian
  spumante (or French
  champagne)

Drop the peaches in boiling water for 30 seconds, take them out and peel them. The contact with boiling water makes the peeling process easier, as the skin will detach from the flesh.

Cut each peach in half and take out the stone. Sprinkle each half with a little icing sugar and let it rest for no more than 5 minutes, or peach will go black. Take four large champagne glasses and arrange in each one 2 peach halves. Fill up the glass with Italian spumante or champagne and serve. Serve with crostoli *(see recipe)*.

Serves 4

Peaches in Spumante

Rock Melon Soup

An unusual dessert which is both light and refreshing.

1 × 750 g rock melon,
  halved and seeded
200 g seedless grapes
200 g apricots, halved and
  stoned
1 medium apple, peeled,
  cored and sliced
1-2 tablespoons lemon juice
3 cups dry white wine
1½ teaspoons cornflour
1 tablespoon honey
75 g pinenuts

Remove flesh from half the rock melon and dice. Using melon baller, scoop flesh from other half. Simmer diced melon, grapes, apricots, apple, lemon juice and wine for 20 minutes. Allow to cool slightly then puree using a sieve, blender or food processor. Return puree to saucepan. Mix cornflour to paste with a little water. Stir cornflour and honey into soup and cook until slightly thickened. Stir in melon balls and chill thoroughly.

Before serving, toast pinenuts by tossing in a dry frying pan until just starting to brown. Ladle soup into 6 bowls and sprinkle with pinenuts. Alternatively, arrange melon balls and pinenuts in individual bowls of soup just before serving.

Serves 6

Banana Cream

100 g dark chocolate
300 mL cream
2 large ripe bananas

Reserve 2 squares of chocolate and melt remainder over hot water. Remove from heat and allow to cool slightly. Whisk cream until thick. Mash bananas and fold with chocolate into cream.

Divide between glasses and grate a little of the reserved chocolate over top of each glass. Chill and serve.

Serves 4

Strawberry Brandy Cream

1 × 810 g can strawberries
⅓ cup cherry brandy
6 teaspoons gelatine
2 cups cream
¼ cup sugar
4 fresh strawberries, hulled
  and chopped, for garnish

Drain canned strawberries reserving the syrup. Combine ¼ cup syrup, brandy and gelatine in a small saucepan and stir. Cook over a low heat until the gelatine has dissolved. Set aside to cool to room temperature.

Whip the cream, add the sugar and continue whipping until soft peaks form. Fold most of the drained strawberries into the cream. Gradually fold in the gelatine mixture and an extra ¼ cup of the reserved syrup. Spoon mixture into a wetted or lightly oiled 4 cup mould. Chill for 3 hours or until set.

Combine the remaining strawberries and syrup in a bowl. Mix with a fork until blended to form a sauce. To serve, unmould Strawberry Cream. Pour syrup over and garnish with chopped strawberries.

Serves 4

Strawberries in Red Wine

400 g fresh strawberries
⅔ cup sugar
1 lemon
1 cup red wine

Hull and wash strawberries, drain carefully and arrange in a glass bowl. Refrigerate for 2 hours. Mix the wine and lemon juice, and add sugar. Stir to dissolve sugar. A little while before serving, pour the wine mixture over the strawberries.

Serves 4

Rock Melon Soup

1. Add wine to fruit mixture and
  simmer for 20 minutes

2. After cooling, puree mixture through
  sieve, blender or food processor

3. Pour cornflour paste and honey into
  puree and cook until thickened

Strawberry Sorbet

1 punnet strawberries
1 cup water
¼ cup sugar
½ cup ice cream
2 tablespoons lemon juice
2 tablespoons kirsch
2 egg whites
¼ cup caster sugar

Wash and hull strawberries. Puree strawberries, water, sugar, ice cream, lemon juice and kirsch. Pour mixture into 2 lamington tins and freeze.

Beat egg whites until stiff. Add caster sugar and beat to dissolve.

Remove strawberry ice from freezer and break up with a fork. Fold egg whites into strawberry mixture and spoon into individual serving bowls. Freeze, stirring every 10 minutes until mixture is firm.

Serves 4

Tamarillo Ice Cream

1 cup sugar
1 cup water
4 tamarillos
1¾ cups cream
3 egg yolks, beaten

Boil sugar and water for 8–10 minutes until thin syrup forms. Add tamarillos and simmer over low heat until just tender. Allow to cool, remove fruit, peel and discard skin. Puree fruit in food processor or blender and strain, discarding seeds.

Bring cream to the boil, add egg yolks and cook over low heat, stirring constantly until mixture coats back of a wooden spoon. Cool and combine with tamarillo puree and syrup. Pour into ice trays and freeze until nearly firm. Stir mixture then freeze until firm.

Serves 4–6

Strawberry Sorbet

Blackcurrant and Orange Ice Cream

250 g blackcurrants
finely grated rind and juice 1
    orange
8 mint leaves
4 tablespoons brown sugar
1¼ cups natural yoghurt
2 eggs, separated
4-6 mint sprigs for garnish

Reserve a few blackcurrants for garnish. Puree remainder in blender or food processor. Add orange rind and juice, mint leaves, sugar, yoghurt and egg yolks and blend until smooth.

Leave in freezer until beginning to thicken and set. Beat egg whites until stiff and fold into ice cream. Freeze until half frozen then beat again. This prevents large ice crystals forming. Freeze until firm. Serve garnished with blackcurrants and mint leaves.

Serves 4

Watermelon Ice Cream

1 cup sugar
2 cups water
250 g watermelon flesh, with
    seeds removed
½ cup cream, whipped

Melt the sugar in 2 cups of warm water and let it boil for 2 minutes. Mash the watermelon flesh and add it to the whipped cream. Fold the watermelon and whipped cream mixture into the cooled syrup. Freeze.

Serves 4

Rhubarb Wine Jelly

450 g rhubarb
2 cups water
2 cups sugar
strip lemon peel
5 teaspoons gelatine
½ cup medium or sweet
    white wine
⅔ cup cream, whipped

Cut the rhubarb in 2.5 cm pieces and cook them for about 25 minutes in the water with the sugar and lemon peel. Remove the lemon peel and strain, reserving the syrup.

Dissolve the gelatine in the syrup and leave to cool. Stir in the wine and rhubarb and chill in a mould until set. Turn out and decorate with whipped cream.

Strawberry Jelly

100 g packet agar-agar	4 egg whites
1 litre water	¼ cup milk
½ cup sugar	1 punnet strawberries
¼ cup plum wine or	
Cointreau	

Break the agar-agar into pieces and place into 1 litre of hot water. Bring to the boil and heat gently for 10 minutes. Add sugar and plum wine and stir until combined and the sugar dissolved. Pour the hot liquid through a strainer and reserve.

Beat egg whites in a bowl until stiff. Fold the egg whites and milk through the warm liquid and pour mixture into a rectangular, plastic mould.

Cut stems off strawberries and arrange in rows in the egg white and agar-agar mixture. Place in refrigerator to set and cool.

When set, cut into squares and serve either on its own or with ice cream or semi-whipped cream.

Serves 6

Strawberry Jelly

Party Cassata

1 litre vanilla ice cream
1 litre chocolate ice cream

Filling

½ cup cream
1 tablespoon angelica,
  chopped
1 tablespoon sultanas
1 tablespoon mixed peel
12 almonds, slivered
12 glace cherries, sliced
2 tablespoons icing sugar

Lightly grease a 1¼-litre mould or pudding basin with oil. Put a disc of oiled foil or paper in the base. Place the basin in the freezer. Soften vanilla ice cream.

Line the prepared mould or basin with the vanilla ice cream, using a round-bowled spoon for spreading. Freeze until firm — about 1 hour. Again work with a spoon to soften the chocolate ice cream, making it pliable. Make a second lining of ice cream in the mould or basin. Cover and freeze until firm.

To make the filling, whip the cream and fold in the prepared fruit and sifted icing sugar. Fill the ice cream-lined mould with the cream-fruit mixture and replace in the freezer.

Take out of freezer about 30 minutes before serving. Turn out with care, and leave in refrigerator for the remaining time before serving.

Serves 8–10

Note: We have made this recipe with vanilla and chocolate ice cream. However, it will be equally delicious made using coffee, strawberry or your favourite flavours.

Date-Avocado Tango

This dish is similar to a mousse, but with more 'goodies'.

2 avocados, mashed
2 tablespoons honey
juice of 1 orange
rind of 1 orange
4 tablespoons chopped dates
½ cup cream, whipped
2 egg whites, stiffly beaten

Mix well avocado, honey, orange juice, rind and dates. Fold whipped cream through (stiffly) and then egg whites (gently) with a metal spoon.

Serve in individual bowls and garnish with very thin strips of orange rind (cooked in honey and water-syrup until soft).

Decorate with more whipped cream around the edges if desired.

Serves 4

Date-Avocado Tango

Frozen Rock Melon and Ginger Mousse

1½ cups rock melon, pureed
½ cup cream, whipped
1 cup fromage blanc (see
   recipe)
1½ tablespoons ginger
   shredded in sugar syrup
⅓ cup sugar
3 egg yolks

Puree the rock melon in a blender, add cream, fromage blanc and ginger. Blend 1–2 seconds. Remove to large bowl.

Whisk sugar and egg yolks over bain-marie until light and creamy and sugar dissolves. Continue whisking until mixture is cool. Fold into rock melon puree. Pour into tray and leave to firm in freezer.

When mixture begins to set, remove to bowl and whisk to increase volume. Return to freezer for 1 hour to set.

Serves 6–8

Charlotte Venezia

225 g dry madeira cake
2 cups chilled coffee
2 tablespoons Tia Maria
1⅓ cups ground almonds
250 g ricotta cheese
1 cup thick cream
2½ tablespoons sugar
few drops vanilla essence

Garnish

3 tablespoons cream,
   whipped
few coffee beans

Cut the madeira cake into slices, 1.25 cm thick. Combine the chilled coffee and Tia Maria in a large bowl. Dip each slice of cake in the coffee mixture so it is well soaked but still firm.

Fry the ground almonds in a lightly greased pan for 3 minutes. Cool on absorbent paper. In a bowl, thoroughly blend the ricotta cheese, almonds, cream, sugar and vanilla essence.

Line a 1 litre pudding basin with the soaked madeira cake, reserving 4 slices for filling. Half-fill the mould with the cream cheese mixture and cover with a layer of cake. Top up with the cream cheese and finish with a layer of cake. Chill for 2 hours or until ready to serve. Turn out and garnish with rosettes of cream and coffee beans.

Serves 6–8

Apricot and Pawpaw Flan

225 g sweet shortcrust pastry
   (see recipe)

Filling

1 cup milk
1 tablespoon cornflour
2 tablespoons sugar
1 egg yolk
5 drops vanilla essence
1 pawpaw
12 canned apricots, halved

Glaze

2½ tablespoons canned
   apricot syrup
2 tablespoons apricot jam
2½ tablespoons sugar
1 tablespoon cornflour

Garnish

¼ cup cream, whipped
5 green glace cherries

Roll out shortcrust pastry and line a greased 20 cm flan case. Bake blind, and cool.

To make the filling: mix a little of the milk with the cornflour and sugar. Heat the remainder in a saucepan. When hot, pour on to the mixture. Stir and return to the saucepan and cook until thick. Remove from heat, stir in the beaten egg yolk, and flavour with vanilla essence. Slice the pawpaw. Add ¼, chopped, to the filling. Pour the filling into the flan case. Arrange the apricot halves and sliced pawpaw on the top.

To make the glaze: boil the apricot syrup, jam and sugar. Add the cornflour mixed with water. Boil for 2 minutes until the glaze clears. Pour over the fruit while warm. Chill. Decorate with stars of whipped cream, using a piping bag and green glace cherries.

Fromage Blanc

100 g cottage cheese
125 g natural yoghurt
3 teaspoons lemon juice

Combine all ingredients and blend until mixture is smooth and thick, like whipped cream. Cover and store in refrigerator for about 12 hours before using.

Makes about 1 cup

Liqueur-Flavoured Apple Fritters

Other fresh fruit such as pear, pineapple or banana may be used in this recipe. Leave fruit to soak in alcohol and sugar before cooking; this breaks down tissues and improves flavour, and they will cook quickly.

3 firm apples (or other fruit)
2 tablespoons sugar
2 tablespoons liqueur
oil for deep frying

Batter

2 cups flour, sifted
pinch salt
1 tablespoon sugar
1 egg, separated
½ cup light beer
½ cup milk and water mixed
1 tablespoon oil or butter

Combine flour, salt, sugar and egg yolk and mix until it resembles breadcrumbs. Gradually add the beer, milk and oil. Transfer to separate bowl, cover and leave in warm place for 2 hours.

Core and slice apples into rings. Sprinkle with sugar and liqueur and leave at least 20 minutes.

Prepare oil for deep frying. With paper towel remove excess moisture from apples.

Add stiffly beaten egg white to batter. Dip fruit in batter and drop immediately into hot oil. Batter will puff in 2–3 minutes. Cook 1–2 fritters at a time and keep the oil at a high temperature. If batter seems too thick, a little water may be added.

Drain on absorbent paper and keep fritters warm until ready to serve. Whipped cream may be served as an accompaniment.

Serves 4

FRITTER FAVOURITES

Fritters are always hot favourites. Make your batter ahead of time and let it rest 1–2 hours to improve the flavour and texture. It may thicken while resting, so add a little more liquid so that it is the right consistency. Fruit should be completely dry before being dipped in the batter. If it's not, the batter won't cling. Drain fruit fritters well and serve immediately.

Deep Fried Ice Cream Balls

1 litre vanilla ice cream
flour, for coating
2 eggs, lightly beaten
2 tablespoons water
½ packet 'Nice' (or similar)
  biscuits, crushed
oil for deep frying

Turn the freezer to the coldest setting. Place two baking trays in the freezer.

Scoop out ice cream balls from the ice cream using a scoop or a tablespoon. Quickly place the ice cream balls on the baking trays and return to the freezer for at least 2 hours.

Place the flour in one dish, beaten eggs and water in another, biscuit crumbs in a third.

Working very quickly, dip the ice cream balls in the flour then the egg and finally the crumbs. Place on the baking trays and return to the freezer. Leave in the freezer for at least 2 hours. (At this stage, the ice cream can be frozen for up to 2 months).

When ready to serve, heat oil for deep frying. Fry the balls, two at a time, until golden brown. Remove immediately and serve with a chocolate or caramel sauce.

Serves 4

Grand Marnier Avocado Crepe

1 quantity sweet crepe batter
4 avocados, thinly sliced

Sauce

3 tablespoons unsalted
  butter
juice of 2 oranges
grated rind of 1 orange
2 tablespoons Grand Marnier
3 tablespoons raw sugar or
  honey

Garnish

whipped cream
thin strips of glazed orange
  slices to garnish

Make crepes and roll into cylinders with avocado slices inside.

Heat butter in frying pan and stir in juice, rind and sugar or honey. Cook a minute or two over a gentle heat.

Add crepe cylinders to sauce and cook gently a little on all sides. Decorate with glazed orange slices. Add Grand Marnier and light with a match. Serve, while alight, with cream in a separate dish.

For 16 crepes

Flambe Fruit

Flambe Fruit

3 mandarins, peeled and
  segmented
4 pears, cut into slices same
  size as mandarin segments
1 cup overproof rum
1 cup brown sugar
4 bananas, peeled and sliced
2 punnets medium-sized
  strawberries, hulled

Place mandarin segments and pear slices in pan, add about ½ cup rum and fold in sugar thoroughly. Heat until the sugar dissolves then add banana slices. When juice starts to bubble add strawberries and stir gently.

Remove pan from heat, warm remaining rum, pour over fruit and ignite, stirring until flame dies down. Serve on a large platter with bamboo forks.

Serves 8–10

Bananas Creole

50 g butter
6 bananas, peeled
3 canned pineapple rings,
  diced
3 tablespoons icing sugar
3 tablespoons syrup from
  canned pineapple
3 tablespoons raisins, soaked
  in 3 tablespoons rum

Melt the butter in a frying pan. Add the bananas and turn them in the butter, over a medium heat, until golden. Add the pineapple and sugar, and cook until the sugar has caramelised. Stir in the pineapple syrup, raisins and rum, heat through and ignite. Serve immediately.

Serves 6

MICROWAVE DINNER PARTY DESSERTS

Marshmallow Pavlova

Base
1 egg white
1 cup icing sugar

Marshmallow
4 egg whites
½ cup caster sugar
¼ teaspoon cream of tartar
300 mL whipped cream
½ cup chopped strawberries
¼ cup almond flakes
1 orange, halved and thinly
    sliced
dark chocolate, melted

TIME: 3 MINUTES

Combine egg white and icing sugar to form a soft dough. Roll out to fit 25–30 cm microwave-safe platter and set aside.

Whisk egg whites for marshmallow pavlova till stiff. Beat in caster sugar and cream of tartar. Ensure that mixture is very stiff. Pipe pavlova mixture around edge of base to form nest shape. Spoon remaining mixture into centre of base. Smooth with knife.

Cook on HIGH 3 minutes. Stand in oven for 5 minutes. Remove and decorate with whipped cream, strawberries, almond flakes, orange slices and piped chocolate. Crushed walnuts and passionfruit also make an attractive garnish.

Serves 8–10

Pecan Chocolate Cake

Pineapple Fruit Salad Meringue

1 firm ripe pineapple
1 × 425 g can fruit salad or
    two fruits, drained
4 tablespoons Cointreau or
    Grand Marnier

Meringue
3 egg whites
½ cup caster sugar
¼ cup toasted almond
    slivers
12 glace cherries

TIME: 3 MINUTES

Cut pineapple in half lengthwise through top. Remove flesh from each pineapple half. Cut out core, dice pineapple into 2 cm pieces and combine with fruit salad and Cointreau. Marinate 15 minutes. Return mixture to pineapple cases.

Beat egg whites until stiff peaks form. Gradually beat in sugar, spread meringue over fruit and top with cherries and almonds. Cook on HIGH 2–3 minutes until set.

Serves 12

Marshmallow Pavlova

Pecan Chocolate Cake

½ cup butter
⅔ cup brown sugar
⅔ cup coconut
⅔ cup chopped pecan nuts
1½ cups flour
1⅓ cups caster sugar
¼ cup cocoa
1½ teaspoons baking
    powder
1 level teaspoon salt
1 cup milk
⅔ cup butter
3 eggs
1 teaspoon vanilla essence

TIME: 19½ MINUTES

Line base of 2 × 22 cm souffle dishes with two rounds of grease-proof paper. Place butter in bowl and cook on high 1½ minutes. Stir in brown sugar, coconut and pecans. Spread mixture evenly in each dish and set aside.

Place remaining ingredients in mixing bowl. Blend at low speed. Beat 2 minutes on medium then divide mixture and spread evenly in each dish. Cook one cake at a time on MEDIUM for 6 minutes then increase to HIGH and cook 2–3 minutes until cake is light and spongy to touch. Let stand 5 minutes.

Turn onto serving plate. Turn second cake out onto the topping side of first cake. Spread any topping which may cling to paper onto cake top.

Serves 8

Chocolate Nut Ice Cream Gateau

Cake

2 cups almond flakes
1 packet chocolate cake mix
60 g butter, melted
2 eggs
½ cup milk
1 tablespoon rum

Ice Cream

6 egg yolks, beaten
2 cups sugar
100 g milk chocolate
1¾ cups icing sugar
1 tablespoon drinking
  chocolate
4 x 300 mL cream, whipped

Garnish (optional)

4 strawberries
1 kiwifruit, peeled and sliced
2 tablespoons cherry brandy

TIME: 25 MINUTES

Combine almond flakes, chocolate cake mix, butter, 2 eggs and milk. Blend together till smooth. Pour batter into a 22 cm cake dish. Cook on MEDIUM 15 minutes. Stand 10 minutes, uncovered.

Crumble cake, add rum to crumbs. Set aside.

Combine egg yolks and sugar in 2 litre casserole dish. Cook on MEDIUM 5–7 minutes. Stir twice. Set aside. Break up chocolate into glass jug. Cook on HIGH 2–3 minutes. Stir.

Sift together icing sugar and drinking chocolate. Fold together egg yolk mixture, melted chocolate, icing sugar, drinking chocolate and cream. Blend evenly.

Press 1 cup cake crumble into 20 cm spring-form cake tin then pour over 2 cups ice cream mix. Repeat layering ¾ cup crumble and 2 cups ice cream finishing with ice cream. Freeze for 6–8 hours.

One hour before serving, carefully release spring-form tin. Mark surface of cake into slices. Decorate with strawberries and kiwifruit. Freeze for 1 hour.

Pour over cherry brandy and serve immediately.

Serves 10–12

1. *Combine almonds, chocolate cake mix, butter, eggs and milk*

2. *Fold together egg yolks, melted chocolate, icing sugar, drinking chocolate and cream*

Grasshopper Torte

⅓ cup butter
1 packet chocolate-flavoured
  plain biscuits, crumbled
4 cups white marshmallows,
  diced
¾ cup milk
¼ cup green Creme de
  Menthe

2 tablespoons white Creme
  de Cacao
2 teaspoons gelatine
2 tablespoons cold water
1 cup stiffly beaten cream

TIME: 3 MINUTES

Place butter in glass bowl and cook on HIGH for 45 seconds. Stir in biscuit crumbs. Put half the mixture into a 23 cm round glass dish. Chill.

Place marshmallows and milk into a large bowl. Cook 1½–2 minutes to melt marshmallows. Stir in Creme de Menthe and Creme de Cacao.

Blend gelatine and water in small bowl. Heat 15 seconds on HIGH. Blend into mixture. Cool. Fold in whipped cream. Pour into crumb-lined dish. Top with remaining crumbs. Chill until firm. Cut into wedges and pipe with whipped cream.

Serves 8

Chocolate Nut Ice Cream Gateau

3. *Layer cake and ice cream mixtures in spring-form tin*

Peaches Italian Style

12 large canned peach halves
12 macaroons, crumbled
2 tablespoons Grand Marnier
300 mL cream, whipped
4 tablespoons toasted
  almond slivers

TIME: 4 MINUTES

Place peach halves in microwave roasting dish. Combine macaroons and Grand Marnier, divide mixture and fill centre of each peach. Cook on MEDIUM 4 minutes or until hot. Before serving top with whipped cream or ice cream and sprinkle with almond slivers.

Serves 12

Strawberries and Kiwifruit in Champagne

1 sugar cube
2 cups champagne
dash nutmeg
36 strawberries, hulled and
  halved
3 kiwifruit, peeled and sliced

TIME: 2 MINUTES

Place sugar cube, champagne and nutmeg in mixing bowl. Cook on HIGH 2 minutes. Stir. Divide fruit equally between 6 parfait glasses. Pour over champagne. Serve chilled.

Serves 6

Fruit Kebabs

3 bananas, thickly sliced
2 apples, cut into chunks
1 pineapple, cubed
2 grapefruit, segmented
1 punnet strawberries,
  halved

Marinade

1 cup orange juice
¼ cup honey
2 tablespoons Cointreau
1 tablespoon brown sugar
1 tablespoon finely chopped
  mint

Mix marinade ingredients together and heat gently to dissolve honey and sugar. Pour over prepared fruit and leave at room temperature 30 minutes. Thread fruit on skewers alternately for colour and grill for about 5 minutes until heated through. Turn and baste frequently.

Serves 6–8

Note: Fruit Kebabs can be made with any fruits in season, just keep colours and flavours in mind as you make your selection.

Strawberries and Kiwifruit in Champagne

INDEX

THE RECIPES

In writing out these recipes, we have selected the easiest and most reliable measuring system for ingredients — metric cups and spoons. In the ingredients list, all spoon and cup measurements are level. We suggest you use a measuring jug for liquids. For convenience we have left butter and fresh fruit measurements in grams.

Standard metric measures

1 cup = 250 mL
1 tablespoon = 20 mL
1 teaspoon = 5 mL

Here are some useful conversions for those who prefer to weigh out their quantities.

Ingredient	Cup	Tablespoon
Butter	250 g	20 g
Cornflour	130	10
Cornflakes	30	
Custard powder	130	10
Desiccated coconut	95	
Flour plain	125	10
self-raising	125	10
wholemeal	135	
Gelatine		12
1 × 10 g envelope will set		
2 cups of jelly		
Mixed peel	175	15
Sugar granulated	250	20
caster	220	20
icing	175	15